DESTINATION:
TEACH FOR AMERICA

DESTINATION:
TEACH
for AMERICA

BUILDING LEADERSHIP

MASTERING THE APPLICATION

ACING THE INTERVIEWS

Jake Whitman

 Pine Street Press

DESTINATION: TEACH FOR AMERICA
BUILDING LEADERSHIP, MASTERING THE APPLICATION,
ACING THE INTERVIEWS

Copyright © 2012 by Jake Whitman

Published by:
Pine Street Press, LLC
P.O. Box 63586
Philadelphia, PA

Printed in the United States of America

ISBN-13: 978-0-9882052-0-8
ISBN-10: 0988205203

Edited by: Christopher Mote and Julia Kantor
Book Design by: Rosamond Grupp

For my parents and my teachers,
the most important and influential guides in my life.

Contents

Introduction

This book is designed to help you get accepted into Teach For America. If you read the book from cover to cover, taking action where needed to build your resume and thoroughly prepare for the application and interviews, your chance of being accepted will increase dramatically. If you pick up the book months or even years in advance, you will be able to build the skills that successful applicants exhibit to convince the selection team that you are the right candidate to lead a classroom. If you open the book two weeks before the deadline, you will get considerable guidance and structure in submitting your application and preparing for the interviews.

There is no easy way into Teach For America. It takes a lot of energy and hard work to develop the types of accomplishments that Teach For America values the most. You must assume leadership positions and do whatever it takes to achieve significant and measurable successes in those roles. You must reach outside your comfort zone and rise to daunting challenges, even if it means that you will sometimes fail. Most importantly, you must be fiercely committed to leading and educating students, and you must showcase that in all parts of your application. This book will help you do all of these things.

Teach For America aligns its selection criteria with those qualities that research has identified in outstanding teachers. The organization has invested heavily in research to determine exactly what differentiates excellent corps members from mediocre ones, and it has incorporated those findings into the applicant evaluation process. Thus, by demonstrating these qualities in your application, as outlined in this book, you will also develop the skills to be an exceptional teacher.

Leadership

The overarching theme of the Teach For America selection process is leadership. All successful corps members[1] are leaders. While exemplary teachers may be introverted or extroverted, male or female, rational or emotional, Teach For America knows that it takes a leader to excel in a classroom, so the program makes sure that all admitted applicants have the potential to become leaders. This doesn't mean that all corps members ultimately succeed in becoming leaders in the classroom, but that they all showed exceptional leadership *potential* in their applications and interviews.

Leadership is a complicated quality. Some define a leader simply as "one who leads" or "one who has followers." Others go much further, delving into the complexities of power, influence, behaviors, visions, values, and inherent traits.

I would like to refer to two quotations that, when combined, I believe form the most accurate definition of leadership in the context of Teach For America's search for exceptional teachers:

1. "Leadership is a function of knowing yourself, having a vision that is well communicated, building trust among colleagues, and taking effective action to realize your own leadership potential."
    —Warren Bennis, pioneer of leadership studies

2. "If your actions inspire others to dream more, learn more, do more, and become more, you are a leader."
    —John Quincy Adams, sixth president of the United States

Bennis deftly defines the practical nature of leadership, while Adams eloquently states the ultimate purpose of a leader. To be an outstanding teacher, you must lead others by creating and communicating a vision among your colleagues (in this case, students), and also inspire those you lead to become more than they could ever imagine. Thus, I will frame leadership according to the following definition, which combines the two aforementioned quotations:

---

1 Teachers in Teach For America are called *corps members*.

Leadership is taking purposeful action in pursuit of an ambitious and well-communicated vision to inspire others to reach and exceed their potential.

Teach For America strives to identify leadership because it is the only universal quality of exemplary corps members. Therefore, keep this crucial question in mind as you read the book and prepare for the application and interviews:

How can I use this knowledge, skill, or quality to demonstrate my leadership potential?

Preparation Timeline

The first part of *Destination: Teach For America* focuses on the organization's mission and selection criteria, and on ways you can improve your candidacy in the months and years before you apply. The second part of the book outlines the recruitment process, application, and interviews, and helps you prepare for each step using the experiences you already have. Your interaction with this book will be very different if you begin reading it one year versus one month before the application is due, but either way you will considerably improve your chance of getting accepted.

Crafting an excellent application starts well before the submission deadline; it takes time to build leadership experiences. As you prepare to submit your application to Teach For America, use the timeline below to ensure that you are staying on track and doing what is necessary to become an exceptional applicant. If you are beginning your preparation late, don't worry; just do as much catching up as you can and focus on crafting the best application possible.

1–2 Years (before the application deadline)

Get involved in an extracurricular activity or organization that you are passionate about	Look for leadership opportunities and take leads on projects	Identify ambitious, desired leadership positions in your organization or elsewhere	Get involved with underserved youth or communities in some capacity

6–12 Months

Run or apply for a leadership position	Sign up for an upper-division class on education and/or poverty	Start deciding whom you will ask for recommendations	Build the qualities and skills of an ideal candidate where possible (Chapters 3 and 4)

3–6 Months

Decide on three individuals whom you will ask for recommendations	Start reading about current trends in the education landscape	Begin learning about Teach For America's mission and vision (Chapter 2)	Fully revamp your online presence (Chapter 5)

1–3 Months

Meet with the recruitment manager on campus	Begin brainstorming your letter of intent	Make a list of all of your significant accomplishments, quantifying them wherever possible

1 Month

Write the first draft of your letter of intent and resume	Start updating your resume	Follow up with the recruitment manager with any additional questions

2 Weeks

Send your letter of intent to multiple people for feedback	Take your resume to your college's career center for review	Practice talking about Teach For America's mission and vision

1 Week

Tell your recommenders that you may be asking for a recommendation soon	Finish the final draft of your letter of intent	Finalize your resume	Carefully check all parts of the application for spelling and grammatical mistakes

Day Before Deadline

Make sure all sections are 100% complete and submit your application. Don't wait until the last day; submit it with plenty of time to spare (and feel free to submit it even earlier)!

PART 1:

Understanding
Teach For America
and Where You Fit In

Chapter 1

Deciding to Apply to Teach For America

Our generation has become more socially aware. The globalization of information has publicly exposed, more than ever, the vast disparities in wealth, status, and education in our society. While some graduates still enter corporate America straight out of college, many more are choosing to spend their early working years making a difference—even more so than in past generations. Because of the heightened awareness, they want to make a positive impact in the world before they get committed to mortgages, marriages, and children. Further, many professionals are deciding to leave successful careers to join movements for social change, even those individuals who do have mortgages, marriages, and children. Often, once people join the fight for equality, they decide to stay for the rest of their lives.

People apply to Teach For America because they want to be a part of our generation's civil rights movement: educational equity. They are tired of seeing the ever-increasing disparity in education in the United States, and they want to do something about it. Teach For America has taken a progressive and innovative role in improving the educational system in our country. The program trains the most talented people it can find to teach relentlessly for two years, and then helps them to either continue their growth as teachers or take their experiences into a new field where they can influence education policy in their own way. Teach For America sees value in both options because it is critical that we improve education from all levels.

Teach For America is not trying to create a new-age teaching school for career teachers. The organization is building a movement of leaders who care about education and will take their experiences with them for the rest of their lives, whether they stay in the classroom as teachers or decide to pursue other occupations. These alumni become doctors who understand low-income children and the importance of communicating with parents. They become state senators who push for progressive education policies to drive funding for schools and pro-student reform. They become principals who develop schools where incredible education takes place. They become consultants who work with education nonprofits and expand their pro bono services to school districts that are in desperate need of restructuring. And yes, they become exemplary teachers who remain dedicated to relentlessly educating their students every year. Teach For America is training the next group of *leaders* in education reform.

The fact that many Teach For America teachers tend to move on from the classroom sparks criticism from opponents. They claim that corps members are cheap labor; that they enter real classrooms to have an "experience" before they go on to make a lot of money as lawyers and doctors; that they are not committed to the children, the teaching profession, or the education movement in general; and that they are simply trying to find their way in the world, treating teaching as an experiment to get to their end goal. After two years, when they are finally starting to get a grasp on their trade, claim the critics, they leave their children behind and are replaced by another "newbie" first-year teacher who has no intention of staying.

While some of these criticisms are valid on the surface—approximately 40 percent of corps members leave the classroom after their second year—we need to again look at Teach For America's objectives. The organization is striving to bring the conversation on education to the forefront of national policy and working to get the strongest leaders on board. If the program can get a future lawyer to defer her acceptance to Columbia Law School and immerse herself in inner-city schools for two years, there is a much greater chance she will work to improve education as a lawyer ten years down the line. Even more importantly, she most likely would never have taught if she had not joined the program—only one in six corps members say they would have become teachers without Teach For America—and yet she is likely to end up staying in education once her commitment ends (according to Teach For America, approximately two-thirds of alumni stay in education in some capacity long-term). Teach For America knows that it takes finding diverse individuals from all backgrounds to drive this movement forward.

Teaching is difficult and exhausting. You will work 16-hour days trying to make your lessons perfect for your students, only to have your plans derailed. You will get cursed at by students and work with teachers who would rather play Solitaire on their computers than teach students during class. You will experience frustrations stemming from seemingly nonsensical policies and bureaucracies that will make you want to throw in the towel.

However, you will also have many days when your students make remarkable gains, both academically and socially. You will have students who inspire you daily with their ingenuity, intelligence, and engaging personalities. You will have students who lean on you for support during difficult times and thank you when they overcome those obstacles. You will learn more than you can imagine from teachers who are incredibly talented, and who have dedicated their lives to the kids and the teaching profession. You will have administrators who are supportive of your energy and innovative ideas, and who will put their necks on the line for you.

The fact is, though, that you will constantly face uphill battles. To be successful, you will work longer hours than your friends in finance and make a fraction of their salaries. The great thing is, you will do this in a dynamic and exciting environment, while making a real difference in the lives of students and contributing to our country's greatest challenge. It is an outstanding way to begin a career.

Benefits and Partnerships

It cannot be denied that Teach For America participants gain invaluable professional opportunities from their time in the corps. I have heard from countless corporate executives, law school admission boards, and top charter school principals how impressed they are with Teach For America alumni. This makes sense, as part of Teach For America's mission is to invest in leaders and fuel long-term impact. The organization wants alumni to use their experiences and skills not only in the classroom and education policy, but in business, medicine, and law as well.

While these partnerships should not be the reason you decide to apply and join if accepted, they are absolutely a positive result of the experience. The following is just a snapshot of the dozens of companies and schools that value the skills gained through the program. You can see the entire list of partnerships on the Teach For America website.[1]

Yale University School of Management

Offers the Teach For America Scholarship, a merit-based scholarship of approximately $20,000, which the school aims to award annually; waives the application fee for all corps members and alumni; offers two-year deferrals to all applicants who choose to join Teach For America.

Harvard University Graduate School of Education

Provides two "Leadership in Education" awards annually for Teach For America alumni enrolling in the full-time master's program. The Leadership in Education Award covers approximately one-half year's tuition.

University of Chicago Law School

Provides $30,000 scholarships for up to five qualified alumni annually; provides one $35,000 scholarship for a qualified alumnus/a pursuing a joint JD/MPP; waives the application fee for corps members and alumni; offers two-year deferrals to applicants who choose to join Teach For America.

Duke University Medical School

Offers two-year deferral for students who are admitted to the program and choose to join Teach For America.

University of Michigan Gerald R. Ford School of Public Policy

Waives the application fee for corps members and alumni. Tuition assistance program has been formally renamed as the Teach For America Fellowship, which provides $10,000 for up to five alumni annually.

New York University Silver School of Social Work

Offers $9,000 scholarships for up to five alumni annually; provides two-year deferral for students who are admitted to the program

---

1 "Graduate School and Employer Partnerships," *Teach For America*, www. teachforamerica.org.

and join Teach For America; waives application fee for exiting corps members who apply during their two-year commitment.

Google

Recruits Teach For America corps members and provides mentorships during their two-year commitment; offers two-year deferrals for students who receive job offers from Google.

McKinsey & Company

Recruits Teach For America corps members; offers two-year deferrals for students who receive job offers from McKinsey and are also accepted into Teach For America.

Deciding to Apply

It takes a lot of work to get accepted into Teach For America, and even more work to perform well in the classroom. Simply reading this book will not help you get accepted; you must act on the suggestions. Before applying, you should also be fully aware of the commitment you will be making if you join the program. Many corps members who do not fully understand the commitment ultimately regret their decision to join the corps, while those who do their research generally excel as teachers.

When thinking about applying, here are some questions to ask yourself:

1. Do I like working with kids?

2. How well do I deal with failure?

3. How well do I deal with stress?

4. How well do I handle obstacles?

5. Can I work well in an unsupervised and unstructured environment?

6. Can I stay calm and collected when things go wrong?

7. Am I able to think on my feet and react to situations in real time?

8. Will I resent taking work home with me, especially when I am not paid overtime?

9. How well do I take constructive feedback from coworkers?

10. How well do I deal with coworkers who have different perspectives than my own?

11. Can I stand by what I know is right, despite what others say?

12. Am I committed to deepening my understanding of the systemic race- and class-based causes of the achievement gap?

13. Am I able to understand how my identity influences my judgments and actions, and actively work to overcome any unintended prejudices and biases?

14. Can I have frank and honest conversations about race and racism to more fully understand and respect the communities and people with whom I will work?

Answer these questions honestly and take some time to consider your responses. If you find yourself answering "no" or "not very well" to a lot of them, then Teach For America may not be a great fit for you. I am not trying to talk you out of applying; I just want you to be aware of the nature of the job. You should only apply if you think you can persevere through these obstacles, reflect honestly on your own background, and continue to be at 100 percent for your students every day, no matter what.

The good news is that Teach For America does a fantastic job of training and supporting corps members. If you feel that you may need work in some areas, Teach For America will be there to help you. You will be given excellent and very targeted instruction during the summer before you start teaching, and you will receive continual support throughout your two years. Ultimately, your success in the classroom is your responsibility, but you will have some of the most dedicated and diligent people in the country helping you work through situations and problems. You will make friends who know exactly what you are going through on a bad day and the exhilaration you feel on a good day. You will become part of a coalition of teachers nationwide working to close the achievement gap.

A Day in the Life of a Corps Member

I want to introduce you to a day in the life of a corps member (CM). Sara was in her second year of teaching high school math in Philadelphia when she offered this account of her routine:

- **6:30 a.m.:** Wake up. I have the luxury of living two blocks away from my school. Waking up this late is not the case for most CMs!

- **7:20 a.m.:** Walk out the door with bag, laptop, lunch, and materials. An easy commute for me—a quick two-block walk. Not having a car and not having to deal with a commute starts my day off with little stress.

- **7:30 a.m.:** Get to school, unload in my classroom, and take care of any preparations (finish up a PowerPoint presentation, print out a worksheet, make copies, set up an activity, help students complete homework/makeup work).

- **8:00 a.m.:** First bell rings, and advisory (homeroom) starts.

- **8:25 a.m.:** First period. I have the first period free, so I spend that time either finishing preparations for the day or starting to prep materials for the next day's lessons. At times, I have meetings with my principal during this period.

- **9:26 a.m.:** Second period. I teach Algebra II.

- **10:21 a.m.:** Third period. During the first semester, I taught a problem-solving class. In the second semester, my third period is an "admin" period, designated for numeracy/math curriculum design. As "math head" of the department, I have meetings with two people who are part of the Drexel University Math Forum (an online math problem-solving program) and/or work to design curricula for a numeracy block, designed to serve the entire school population starting in fall 2012.

- **12:06 p.m.:** Fourth period. I teach another Algebra II class.

- **1:01 p.m.:** Fifth period, which is my lunch. During lunch, I normally have kids stay for makeup work or just to hang out, so I rarely get a true lunch break. For 11 weeks starting in mid-January, I held an initiative on emotion regulation and mindfulness every Tuesday and Thursday with a group of 12 students.

- **1:56 p.m.:** Sixth and seventh periods. I teach two more classes of Algebra II.

- **3:30 p.m.:** The final bell rings. I usually stay at school until about five o'clock to help students with extra work, meet with teachers/principal, chat with students, or make preparations for the next day.*

- **6:00 p.m.:** I get back to my apartment (except on grad school days**). I either make dinner or pick up food, if I am too exhausted to go grocery shopping, and usually spend the rest of the night working on stuff for my classes, whether that means talking to a student on the phone, making a quiz/test/ homework assignment, planning lessons and units, or getting materials ready for the next day. I spend a lot of my time on TFANet or Google, trying to find decent resources to use in my classroom. In my first year, most of my time was spent researching these resources and aligning them to fit in my classroom.

- **10:00 p.m.–midnight:** I am good at getting my sleep! Some nights, I'd be in bed as early as ten, but there were plenty of nights I wouldn't get to bed until midnight or later.

*From December to early February, I co-coached girls' JV basketball. We would have practices/games after school. Practices were normally two or three times per week, and we had games twice per week. Practice ran 4:00 p.m.–6:00 p.m., and games were usually over by five.

**If it is a grad school day, I head straight to UPenn after school, where I have class either 5:00 p.m.–7:00 p.m. or 5:00 p.m.–8:00 p.m.
—Sara Kuzmik (Philadelphia '10)

How to Maintain a Healthy Lifestyle

Great teachers keep long hours. Forget about those people who argue that teachers have it easy because they get two months and all federal holidays off. If you want to be a great teacher, you will occasionally work upward of 80 hours per week, and you will certainly work on weekends, whether from home or at school. That lifestyle takes a toll on your health, both physically and mentally.

To maintain your energy, it is imperative that you find time for your personal needs. We all have needs that are vital to our mental and physical health, so make sure you are able to budget them into your busy schedule. One key to staying healthy is setting personal goals and boundaries and enforcing them. If you know you need to get seven hours of sleep to function the next day, make sure that you schedule your day so you can be in bed by 10:30 p.m. If you know you need to exercise four times per week, schedule it around your other commitments and stick to it. You obviously cannot do everything you want to do, but if you plan it out strategically, you will strike a balance between work and leisure that best suits your needs.

Teach For America makes a point of addressing this issue with incoming corps members. The staff knows that tired and burned-out teachers make poor teachers, and they want to help you stay energized and mentally strong. During Institute,[2] along with sessions on pedagogy and classroom management, you will receive practical recommendations on staying healthy while in your placement city. Don't blow these off as unimportant, even though you will be tired and tempted to zone out during these presentations. You may be more thankful for some of these recommendations than anything else you learn all summer. The Teach For America staff members have been in your shoes and have learned how to maintain a balanced lifestyle, a skill that is more important than you can imagine.

---

2 *Institute* refers to the five-week training all corps members receive prior to entering the classroom.

Leading a Healthy Lifestyle as a Corps Member

When I realized the importance of my job as a corps member, I knew that I would have to make some lifestyle changes in order to best reach the children that needed me on a daily basis. Figuring out how to lead a healthy lifestyle allowed me to perform at a high level in my classroom and in graduate school, all while still maintaining a strong social life.

Exercise 4–5 times a week. In my first year of teaching, I was fortunate enough to live with four other CMs who were dedicated to doing whatever it took to provide students with what they needed. In order to maintain that level of energy, we started a challenging workout regimen and held each other accountable for maintaining it. Our regimen required us to be in the gym for one to two hours most weekdays, regardless of how tired we were. Regular exercise not only led to an increase in energy, but also provided us with an opportunity to step away from it all.

Maintain a healthy diet. Arguably, the most important switch I made in my time as a corps member was the switch to a healthy diet. The great thing is that learning about healthy nutrition not only ensured that I would be ready for my students each morning, but also allowed me to instruct my students on living healthy. By the end of our health unit, I had fourth graders running up to me to brag that they had snacked on baby carrots instead of potato chips.

Find your working style and stick to it. Not everyone works the same way, and there isn't one single correct working style. In my house of five CMs, every one of us went about our jobs differently, and every one of us was successful in leading our students to high achievement. If you know that your body requires a lot of sleep, put yourself in a position to get that sleep. I was able to get at least eight hours of sleep each night because that's what I needed in order to be a great teacher. I remember feeling guilty at first that I wasn't working as many hours as my roommates, but I compensated by working efficiently to maximize my time.

Take time for yourself. I think that this is the most important of all the guidelines that I follow. As a teacher, you have an endless list of tasks to complete, and you could work 20 hours a day and still find more to do. By taking time for yourself, you will be a much happier teacher, and happier teachers are usually better when they get in front of their kids.

—Bill Fickett (Las Vegas '10)

Summary

Joining the program is a unique opportunity to have a tremendous impact in the short-term, and to develop leadership skills to shape education for the rest of your life. It is difficult to develop the skills that Teach For America values the most in its selection process because the organization wants to ensure that it only selects the highest-quality candidates. However, while it is difficult to exemplify the qualities that Teach For America uses in selection, it is not impossible; it just takes hard work.

Your job, if you are accepted, will be exhausting but fulfilling. While nothing can fully prepare you for stepping into the classroom that first day, with this book and the guidance of Teach For America, you will be ready to teach your students.

With all of this in mind, let's take a more in-depth look at the mission of Teach For America.

Chapter 2

Teach For America's Mission and Vision

Your first step before applying to Teach For America is to understand and internalize fully the organization's mission, vision, and values. Woven throughout the application and interviews during the selection process will be questions designed to give you room to demonstrate that you know what Teach For America stands for, and that you believe strongly in the mission. The selection team must know that you understand that teaching children growing up in poverty is not something to be taken lightly. If you are accepted, you will be in charge of students who need teachers willing to do virtually anything to ensure that they learn. This is as important as anything else in the evaluation process.

This chapter will go through each part of the mission in depth and explain how Teach For America is working to achieve those goals. In addition to reading this chapter, you should spend some time on the Teach For America website, learning how the organization talks about its mission. You should be able to explain the mission in your own words in 10 minutes or sum it up in 10 seconds, depending on the situation. Talk to your friends, family, and peers about the organization and try to relate Teach For America's mission to your own values and experiences.

When reading this chapter, think about Teach For America's mission and vision in terms of leading children to success. Consider how you can use the organization's message to empower yourself and your students to achieve exceptional results. When you finish reading this chapter and browsing the website, spend some time internalizing it and thinking about what Teach For America means to you.

Mission

Teach For America is growing the movement of leaders who work to ensure that kids growing up in poverty get an excellent education.[1]

This statement is the crux of Teach For America. Above anything else, Teach For America was established to help ensure that all students in our country receive an excellent education. Corps members are expected to prevail against every obstacle and lead students to success in their classrooms. If accepted into the movement, you will be expected to teach your students at a high level no matter what—no excuses.

Notice that the mission does not even include the word "teacher." It is a movement of *leaders*, plain and simple. It is this emphasis on leadership that differentiates Teach For America from other paths to the classroom and has made Teach For America teachers so successful in ensuring that their students receive an excellent education.

A Solvable Problem

The education achievement gap is something that can be eliminated. Cities and regions that have decided to focus on student achievement above all else, and have done so effectively, have seen tremendous boosts in literacy scores, graduation rates, and college matriculation. Many high-performing charter schools have been established in low-income neighborhoods and now send 100 percent of their graduating students to college. Countless teachers have helped low-income students grow at seemingly impossible rates in just a year's time. The question is no longer a misguided, "Can students living in poverty learn?" but rather, "How can we work to ensure educational equity for all?"

A strong teacher, a positive support structure, and high expectations can overcome even the most crippling of obstacles for students. As many corps members will proudly exclaim, a student's zip code does not preclude him from learning. Low-income students have the same capacity to learn as their more fortunate peers, and when in the classroom of an exemplary teacher, they will perform at the same high levels.

Let's take a look at examples of excellence at three different levels: a city, a charter school network, and an individual teacher.

---

1 "Our Mission," *Teach For America*, www.teachforamerica.org.

New Orleans

The city of New Orleans has faced a unique set of challenges in its efforts to close significant gaps in student achievement levels over the past decade. The destruction wrought by Hurricane Katrina, and the subsequent rehabilitation and reconstruction of the city, provided a rare opportunity to meaningfully reform the city's educational institutions. Within weeks of the hurricane, education advocates and reformers realized that, despite the remarkable scale of the student achievement gap in New Orleans before the hurricane, an opportunity to implement initiatives and interventions aimed at addressing that gap had finally arrived.

As New Orleans began the daunting task of rebuilding societal institutions and structures that essentially had been destroyed, citizens, government bodies, and NGOs rallied around the development effort. Many of these stakeholders agreed that innovation in rebuilding the city's education system was critical. The city charged Paul Vallas, a national education reformer who became renowned for his leadership at the Louisiana Recovery School District (RSD), with enacting strategic and operational reform initiatives that New Orleans public schools required so desperately. Under Act 35, passed during a special session of the Louisiana Legislature following the hurricane, Vallas and the RSD were given five years to successfully implement those reform initiatives in 107 of the 116 New Orleans public schools.[2]

Vallas and the RSD enjoyed remarkable success in their efforts to rebuild New Orleans' education system and close the student achievement gap, though not without sparking controversy. For example, the decentralization of power between the Orleans Parish School Board (OPSB) and the RSD inflamed certain vested-interest groups and stakeholders, yet has been credited with reducing patronage and increasing partnership and collaboration.[3] In the larger national debate

---

2 Horne, Jed. 2011. "New Schools in New Orleans: School Reform Both Exhilarated and Imperiled by Success," *Education Next*; Recovery School District Legislatively Required Plan 8. 2006. 12.

3 Holley-Walker, Danielle. 2007. "The Accountability Cycle: The Recovery School District Act and New Orleans' Charter Schools," *Connecticut Law Review* 40(1):147.

regarding school choice, the RSD has overseen the transformation of New Orleans into the United States' first majority-charter school district.[4]

RSD reforms, which place an emphasis on performance-based accountability, have proven to be particularly effective in narrowing the achievement gap for students of color and low-income students. Before Hurricane Katrina, a 50.6-point gap in English standardized test scores and a 52.8-point gap in math standardized test scores existed between black and white students in New Orleans public schools.[5] These gaps were twice as large as the gaps in standardized test scores between black and white students in all other districts of Louisiana.[6] By 2011, this gap had narrowed significantly to 42 percent.[7]

In 2011, 53 percent of black New Orleans students performed at grade level on standardized tests, as opposed to 32 percent that had done so in 2006.[8] Among New Orleans students with special needs, 36 percent performed at grade level in 2011, as opposed to 16 percent that had done so in 2007.[9] While these numbers are admittedly not at an ideal level, they show tangible progress in a remarkably short time period.

Teach For America has been critical to the successful implementation of the performance-based innovations at the center of New Orleans' education reforms. Kira Orange Jones, a 2000 South Louisiana corps member and the regional executive director of Teach For America, simultaneously quadrupled the number of corps members on the ground in the aftermath of Katrina and doubled the number of alumni.[10]

While there is still much to be done, data shows that progress is continuing in New Orleans, despite continued opposition to the RSD's

---

4 Chang, Cindy. 2011. "Recovery School District's Paul Vallas to Help Overhaul Schools in Chile," *The Times-Picayune*.

5   Recovery School District Legislatively Required Plan 8. 2006. 9.

6   Ibid.

7   Vanacore, Andrew. 2011. "New Orleans Public School Achievement Gap Is Narrowing," *The Times-Picayune*.

8   Ibid.

9   Ibid.

10   "Greater New Orleans-Louisiana Delta," *Teach For America*, www. teachforamerica.org.

methods. Partnership and collaboration among teachers, communities, nonprofits, and students have been crucial to these successes, and have come to exhibit nationwide how real progress can be obtained. If you want to work in the heart of education reform, consider choosing New Orleans as your highest-priority region when you apply.

YES Prep

There are countless examples of charter schools and networks that educate low-income students at the same level as their affluent peers. Often, these exceptionally high-performing charter schools will take perpetually failing students and lead them to extraordinary improvements. The Knowledge Is Power Program (KIPP) is perhaps the best-known charter network to achieve these results, but there are many more that have shown exceptional success with their students.

YES Prep is a high school charter network in Houston, Texas. YES Prep sees 100 percent of its graduates accepted into four-year colleges or universities. In fact, a college acceptance letter is a stipulation for receiving a diploma, and students who are not accepted to a college must stay an extra year at YES Prep (this happens on rare occasions). Overall, 99 percent of YES Prep students graduate, compared to 63 percent in Houston as a whole, and the school's proficiency rates in reading, math, writing, science, and social studies are all above 95 percent. And in case you were wondering, 80 percent of the students are economically disadvantaged, and 95 percent are African-American or Hispanic. This school has methodically eliminated any argument that students in low-income communities cannot be successful in the classroom.

In 2011, I attended a panel discussion titled "The Culture of Leadership," in which Chris Barbic, the founder of YES Prep and a Teach For America alumnus, participated alongside several other education leaders. Barbic's answer to one question in particular will stick with me forever. The moderator asked, "Chris, what is the most important part of this puzzle of building an organization with hyper-successful outcomes?" Without hesitating, Barbic said, "The people." This response reveals why Teach For America is so focused on selecting the best individuals to lead students. Rather than investing in curricula, technology, or other educational resources, the organization devotes time, money, and energy to selecting people with strong leadership potential and then rigorously and methodically training them to teach.

Geoff Kozak (Philadelphia '09)

Geoff grew up in a small town near Penn State University and attended Carnegie Mellon University. As a corps member, Geoff taught in a discipline school, Camelot Excel South, in Northeast Philadelphia. Most of his students had either been expelled from their neighborhood schools or incarcerated. Excel South is somewhat of a "last chance" for students who could not succeed in a traditional school environment. His students were pegged by society as young adults who could not learn and would almost inevitably end up in prison. Geoff proved everyone wrong.

Geoff taught chemistry, the most difficult science for high school students to master (even adults cringe at the mention of the class), but one that is required for graduation. At the beginning, many of his students ignored him when he announced that he was no longer going to let the school district fail them. They were admittedly frustrated with the education that had been provided to them thus far. But Geoff accepted no excuses and used every second of his time effectively. As he maintained a positive outlook and unrelentingly high expectations throughout the year, his students grew to love him for his constant demand for success. Those same students who had cursed at him at the beginning of the year later told him that he was the best teacher they had ever had. One of his former students spoke at her class's graduation and shouted him out, not for being her favorite teacher or the most fun one, but for "challenging me to realize my full potential."

In his two years in the corps, Geoff's students reached 90 percent mastery on the state standards in chemistry.[11] This means that his students did not just adequately learn the subject, they became experts in it. Geoff was named Teacher of the Year for all 18 Camelot schools nationwide, schools based everywhere from Philadelphia, Pennsylvania, to Pensacola, Florida, to DeKalb, Illinois. He also won the Sue Lehmann Award for Excellence in Teaching, a Teach For America award that

---

11 The standard benchmark for success in Teach For America is 80 percent mastery of state standards in a subject.

recognizes extraordinary second-year teachers in urban and rural public schools. While not a single moment of his time as a teacher was easy, he proved that an outstanding teacher can overcome and far surpass the status quo.

I asked Geoff to write a narrative that describes his teaching philosophy. The pages at the end of this chapter delve into the mind of one of the top corps members in the country in 2009–2011. I urge you to take special note of his advice for staying positive and focused on what is ultimately all that matters: the students.

Enlisting Committed Individuals

Teach For America is looking for the highest caliber individuals to lead classrooms. When you apply, you will compete against student body presidents, Harvard debate team leaders, experienced professionals, and even former Army sergeants. The average college grade point average (GPA) of Teach For America corps members is 3.6. Virtually all have done something that would make them stand out in most job interviews.

But there's something else that Teach For America is looking for: people who are *committed* to a cause. The program wants people who have persevered through difficult times and demonstrated passion in their efforts. Teach For America's selection process, which will be highlighted in Part 2 of this book, digs deep to find this quality. You can have a perfect GPA and a number of extracurricular and volunteer activities on your resume, but if you haven't demonstrated a commitment to your endeavors, especially in the face of difficult challenges, you are not worth the program's investment.

Successful Teach For America teachers have a fire burning behind every action they take, and they never quit fighting for what they believe. Great corps members don't care about excuses, uncooperative administrations, or poor conditions. Instead, they constantly reflect on what they can control and improve their craft to overcome obstacles that are preventing progress. They are going to teach their students to read critically and perform long division as if the kids' lives depend on it (which they do). As an applicant, you need to find that grit and determination in yourself and know that it is imperative to stay committed throughout your two years.

Investing in Leaders

As I mentioned in Chapter 1, Teach For America is not necessarily a pipeline for career teachers, but it is a pipeline for the engaged future leaders of our nation. The organization spends tens of thousands of dollars on each corps member every year because Teach For America truly believes it is investing in the leaders that our education system needs. The organization provides intensive training, comprehensive support, and ongoing career development to ensure that each corps member has the necessary tools to help close the achievement gap in the classroom.

Leaders facilitate growth. Leaders do not tell other people what to think or force them to action. Rather, they influence others to join their side and help those people buy into their beliefs and objectives. A good leader's goals become the goals of her followers because she is passionate, honest, and firm in her convictions. Strong leaders have their own "personal brand" to which others subscribe. This concept is as true when leading a classroom of children as it is when leading a company or an entire country.

Leadership is heavily emphasized throughout the entire two-year program. From your first day in Institute, you are charged with leading your classroom to success. In a school setting, strong leaders forge a culture of integrity, consistency, and accountability. In a classroom, leadership is often the one quality that sets exceptional teachers apart from average or even good ones. There is a reason that corps members are called "teacher-leaders" during Institute. Teach For America does not just want teachers to instruct the students; the program wants teachers to help students internalize their learning, set goals for themselves, and track their own upward progress. These are the same strategies used by successful top-level executives at Fortune 500 companies to lead and motivate their employees and managers.

Fueling Long-Term Impact

There are currently 28,000 Teach For America alumni in the United States, and some 5,000 more will join their ranks next summer. The majority of these alumni have stayed in the education field in some capacity. Many have gone on to accomplish truly amazing things. Teach For America alumni have started schools, run for public office, advocated for education policy, and founded education-related nonprofits. Others have remained as teachers and intend to stay in the profession long-term. And many of those who have not remained in the field of education per se have stayed connected and actively involved in the movement—as lawyers who focus their practices on education, doctors who work in low-income hospitals, or journalists who push their companies for more exposure of education issues.

Opponents of Teach For America claim that teachers who leave the classroom after two years hurt schools and students. Yet, as you can see from the following list—a very brief snapshot of the alumni network—the long-term, "macro" impact of the program far outweighs any potential harm, even when discussing those who did not remain in the classroom.

Michelle Rhee (Baltimore '92)

Former superintendent of the Washington D.C. School District and executive director of StudentsFirst, a 501(c)(4) organization, which is building a national movement to defend the interests of children in public education

Mike Feinberg and David Levin (Houston '92)

Co-founders of the Knowledge Is Power Program (KIPP), a high-impact charter school network that consistently achieves exemplary results with its students and trains them to succeed in college

Sekou Biddle (New York '93)

Member of the District of Columbia State Board of Education and former executive director of Jumpstart Washington DC, an organization that builds language and literacy skills in preschool students

Jason Kamras (Washington, D.C. '96)

Chief of the Office of Human Capital for D.C. Public Schools, who was named National Teacher of the Year in 2005

Avi Cover (Washington, D.C. '96)

Director of the Urban Revitalization Program at Seton Hall University's Center for Social Justice, where he teaches law students how to use the legal system to alleviate poverty

Michael Johnston (Mississippi Delta '97)

State legislator in the Colorado State Senate and policy advisor for New Leaders for New Schools

Jocelyn Lewis (New York City '99)

Therapy program manager at SunDance Rehabilitation Corporations, where she works directly with children

Pearl Chang Esau (Los Angeles '03)

CEO of Expect More Arizona, a nonprofit education-advocacy group, and chair of the Arizona Public Engagement Task Force

Brad Allen (New York City '07)

National growth director for Inspire, Inc., a pro bono consulting firm for nonprofits

Brian Bordainick (New Orleans '08)

Founder and executive director of the 9th Ward Field of Dreams in New Orleans, a $1.85 million community space with football field and track, open to the public free of charge

Alejandro Gac-Artigas (Philadelphia '09)

Founder of Springboard Collaborative, an incentive-based summer enrichment program that eliminates the reading gap among low-income students

It is too early to tell how the expanding alumni network will continue to influence education reform. Though some will abandon education altogether, I have no doubt that the vast majority will have a meaningful, positive effect on education throughout their chosen careers. As the years go on, those alumni will be older, more experienced, and more influential. They will be teachers, policy makers, and social workers. They will lead education social ventures and represent students in the courtroom. They will influence legislation, create excellent schools, and continue to fight for equity in education.

Vision

One day, all children in this nation will have the opportunity to attain an excellent education.[12]

Teach For America's long-term goal is to cease to exist, to render itself defunct. In an ideal world, there would be no achievement gap. Students from all socioeconomic backgrounds, races, ethnicities, and religions would have the same opportunity for an excellent education. Unfortunately, we are still far from that utopia, but Teach For America continues to lead the charge in that direction. While total numbers are still relatively insignificant, by 2021 there will be more than 100,000 corps members and alumni.

We need the smartest people in the country to be personally involved in the movement, and Teach For America gives individuals personal experiences to draw on for the rest of their lives. Only when education reform becomes truly progressive and the status quo allows for more innovative and efficient processes will this vision be fulfilled. Success requires recruiting great people to lead our students in the classroom and supporting leaders in politics, law, business, medicine, nonprofits, and many other fields to affect positive change in their respective practices.

---

12 "Vision," *Teach For America*, www.teachforamerica.org.

Just Teach the Kids

I didn't know what to expect as I entered Teach For America, as I blindly and excitedly committed to the program. There weren't any corps members from my hometown or from Carnegie Mellon, where I went to college, so I didn't have a reference to discuss their experience. For some reason, I both assumed that I would and wanted to be placed in the worst possible situation I could have envisioned: locked in a classroom with thirty high schoolers without any support from principals, administrators, co-teachers, parents, teacher coaches, etc. Any change was going to be a result of the relationship between my students and me. I thought it was going to be like a team. I was the captain/teacher and our team/classroom was going to win a championship/embrace learning. I hoped for this challenge, for that's what I thought I was choosing to do. I thought that this setting was the one where the most change could be made.

After completing Institute, I was initially placed in two different schools before the start of the academic year. Both were large, comprehensive high schools where my perfectly envisioned situation could fall into place. However, one of the schools already had a chemistry teacher and the other had no idea who I was (obviously, either Teach For America (TFA) or the School District of Philadelphia mishandled my situation). But I was OK with this mishap because I anticipated the worst possible scenarios.

I remember other corps members being completely uneasy without a placement, but I was OK with not knowing. I even tried to embrace not knowing. The day before school was to begin, my program director (PD) called me and asked if I wanted to be a science teacher at a new discipline school in Northeast Philly. He thought that I had the personality to handle students who had been either incarcerated or expelled from their neighborhood public schools. To this day, I don't know if he talked me up because he sincerely thought that I could handle the setting or because he was just trying to place me somewhere. Nonetheless, I enthusiastically accepted my placement and began day one of the school year.

I mention this because I think a positive, open mindset going into TFA is as essential as anything else in terms of succeeding in the classroom. Leadership qualities, ability to problem solve, relentless pursuit, etc., are all important characteristics that make a quality teacher—and ones that TFA values—but a corps member has to have a positive outlook from the outset, both before and after his placement, and avoid a negative mindset at all costs. Regardless of my situation, I knew that I was going to start at the exact same baseline: primarily me as the teacher, my students as the learners, and everyone else involved as ancillary components. If all corps members had this mindset, I feel that TFA would be in a better place.

My approach to teaching was not a complex, involved strategy. I used some of the methods and techniques from TFA, Penn Graduate School of Education, and other corps members, but my main approach to the two-year commitment was a culmination of three factors. The first was my mindset going into the program, as explained above, in hoping for the worst possible situation, where my sole purpose for two years was to teach students about chemistry and the value of learning. I was committed to that (after all, we all do sign up for a two-year *commitment*). My two years weren't going to be about me and my development. I had already been given opportunities in my life. It was going to be about my students.

The second factor was hearing my first-ever students at Institute tell me story after story of teachers not caring and simply not teaching them what they had anticipated they were going to learn. Kids want to learn. My 17-year-olds from Northeast Philadelphia wanted to learn. All they wanted was for a teacher to teach them. And the third factor, to be quite honest, came from some other corps members and teachers complaining every day about how they had a tough placement, how Student X did this and Student Y did that, how they had to teach two different subjects, or how their PD didn't give them enough one-on-one support. I found the complaining ridiculous, and I know it was detrimental to their being effective.

These three factors led me to a phrase that I still believe is the most important mindset for a corps member to have: "Just f@$*ing teach the kids." The first time I used that phrase was when I was talking to my PD and a few other TFA "higher-ups." My PD was saying how I was doing an effective job, and they were asking what it was that made me effective. Eventually, after describing my classroom culture and trying to discuss my teaching qualities, I finally said to them that all we have to do is "just f@$*ing teach the kids," adding, "It's unbelievable to me how so many corps members and district teachers complain about students and administrators and rarely take the blame themselves." I felt that my students' learning was completely on me. Even if there were many external factors, I had no control over those, so I didn't worry about them. I simply had their time whenever they were in my classroom. That's it. Perhaps I was a little too frank, but I think they got the point.

So, I took this approach to my classroom every single day, every single period, every single minute. I taught this way in a cafeteria, an old, converted swimming pool, and a trailer (all "classrooms" during my two years). I took this approach from the first period on Monday morning to after lunch on Friday afternoon. I used it on the days before Christmas break and days after state testing, when the school year was, by many people's calculations, "over." I used it in the first several weeks, when I was told to "f@$* off" by several students and months later when those same kids told me that I was the best teacher they ever had. I taught with this approach when I was sick. I even tried to have my substitutes use it when I was away for medical school interviews.

When my students walked through the door, it was time to learn. Literally, from the first second to the last, my students were doing something. It was nonstop from beginning to end. The classroom motto was, "No excuses, get it done." My students sometimes struggled with this approach, coming from other classrooms and because our periods were 70 minutes long. But I didn't care. If a kid was disruptive, I would try to calm him or her down (which often worked). If it didn't and the disruptiveness continued, I sent him or her out of the classroom, which was rare (I had the principal's backing on this because she knew that if a kid was ever kicked out of my classroom, it was for disrupting the learning environment). There were no excuses.

I would talk to those disruptive kids after class, at lunch, or the next day; it wasn't for me to apologize for sending them out, but rather to tell them that their behavior simply wasn't appropriate and I expected more. They had been cheated out of a legitimate education for many years, and I wasn't going to let it happen again, at least not in my classroom. I challenged them, I encouraged them, and I yelled at them. I was relentless and had high expectations. Things weren't always easy. Those two years were probably the two most stressful years of my life, but it wasn't about me. I was exhausted at the end of every single day, but the kids didn't see that. I couldn't let them see that. It was about my students and what they were capable of learning.

They eventually mastered 90 percent of the material. I used questions from the New York State Regents Exam, from the SAT II Chem test, and from other high-level standardized exams. I claimed throughout the entire year that if you failed my final, then you failed my course. The final was cumulative. From day one, I counted down the number of days until the final. My students accepted the challenge, as most people would. I had them work on public speaking by filming them in front of the class and then subsequently critiquing them in front of their peers. Because the classroom culture was all about learning and progress, students were happy to participate, both in accepting and providing criticism. Students were so eager to learn more chemistry that I asked my principal if I could start a Chem II class in my second year. She happily agreed. My kids succeeded, and I use the term "success" to mean they learned to value education, efficiency, time management, team success, and even chemistry.

So, my message to incoming corps members, just as it was in my classroom, is: "No excuses, get it done." Please, just f@$*ing teach the kids.

—Geoffrey Kozak (Philadelphia '09)

Chapter 3

The Ideal Applicant

Teach For America is very transparent about the qualities, or "core competencies," that it looks for in applicants. The selection team wants to know not only that you are smart, but also that you can overcome challenges and become a true leader in the classroom. Teach For America has spent a lot of time and money learning what makes a great teacher, and these qualities have been used to create the selection criteria.

Specifically, the ideal applicant exhibits the following seven qualities, taken directly from Teach For America's website.[1] The selection team weights all seven of these core competencies equally when evaluating applicants:

1. A deep belief in the potential of all kids and a commitment to do whatever it takes to expand opportunities for students

2. Demonstrated leadership ability and superior interpersonal skills to motivate others

3. Strong achievement in academic, professional, extracurricular, and/or volunteer settings

4. Perseverance in the face of challenges, ability to adapt to changing environments, and a strong desire to do whatever it takes to improve and develop

5. Excellent critical thinking skills, including the ability to accurately link cause and effect and to generate relevant solutions to problems

---

1 "Who We Look For," *Teach For America*, www.teachforamerica.org.

6. Superior organizational ability, including planning well and managing responsibilities effectively

7. Respect for individuals' diverse experiences and the ability to work effectively with people from a variety of backgrounds

But what does each of those qualities really mean? What kind of leadership is the organization looking for? How can it measure your respect for diverse backgrounds? This chapter will define each of the seven qualities, explain how the Teach For America selection team evaluates them in applicants, and show you how to exhibit them in your application.

Quality 1: Belief and Commitment

A deep belief in the potential of all kids and a commitment to do whatever it takes to expand opportunities for students

The first part of this quality is essentially the topic of Chapter 2— understanding Teach For America's mission and vision. You must show the interviewers that you have internalized Teach For America's values and that they will drive you to succeed in educating your students. You have to know that closing the achievement gap is a matter of putting the time and energy into teaching your students at a high level every day, no matter what obstacles you face.

The best way to exhibit "a deep belief in the potential of all kids" is to learn as much as you can about Teach For America, the achievement gap, and the education landscape as a whole. Since the previous chapter is dedicated to this topic, I simply want to reiterate the importance of understanding the mission and vision of Teach For America.

The second half of this quality, "a commitment to do whatever it takes to expand opportunities for students," deserves a bit more explanation. Teach For America used to refer to this as the quality of being "relentless." While they no longer use this term as one of the seven competencies, I still think it best exemplifies the quality for which the organization searches.

Relentlessness means forcibly driving toward solutions to problems. It means doing whatever it takes to accomplish what is right. It means being so committed to your goal that you will stop at nothing to ensure its success. There are times you must be unyielding and strict to get over a difficult hurdle. It can be hard to be inflexible, but it is essential to be so at times to change the status quo. After all, the status quo is why the achievement gap exists.

As a teacher, you will often have to be relentless simply to give your students the opportunities they deserve. You might have classes where students have a wide variety of needs, both academically and emotionally, and you will have to ensure that every need is met. You may have to teach content at an eighth-grade level while addressing third-grade concepts that students never mastered. You might have to work with students to overcome barriers that they face as a result of poverty. All of these require you, as a teacher, to relentlessly pursue success until it is obtained.

Other times, you might have to be relentless when advocating for a student. As a special education teacher, I sometimes had to fight tooth and nail with my administration to switch my kids out of a class where a teacher was unwilling to put in the extra work to accommodate my students' learning styles. While it is a minority of teachers and administrators who exhibit a lack of effort to this degree, it is a larger minority than we would like to see, and it is this minority that often makes progress difficult from an organizational level. Corps members do everything they can to ensure that they overcome these challenges.

Exhibiting This Quality

Teach For America is not necessarily interested in hearing about how you were relentless in an education setting. The selection team knows that most applicants have little or no experience in the classroom. They really want to hear that you were heavily committed to something, so much so that you did whatever it took to accomplish your goal. They want to hear that you took a risk, that you rebounded from obstacles stronger than before, and that you were relentless in your approach to a problem. They want to hear that a challenge seemed impossible at first, but that you took action and ultimately succeeded.

Examples of relentlessness can be hard to find because, quite frankly, we are not asked to be relentless all that often in college. Think creatively about times you have worked in this unyielding manner. If you were a volunteer or paid staff member on a political campaign, did you take any actions that seemed unbelievably harsh but were necessary to help your candidate succeed? If you volunteered with a nonprofit, did you ever have an idea that was immediately shut down by your superior? What did you do to convince him otherwise? Make sure you think long and hard to find an example and be ready to show that you can take action when needed.

Quality 2: Leadership and Interpersonal Skills

Demonstrated leadership ability and superior interpersonal skills to motivate others

Leadership

As mentioned in the introduction, Teach For America's goal is to find future leaders. While past leadership experience is one strong indicator of whether a candidate will be a leader in the future, this core competency is not weighted more heavily in the selection criteria than any of the others. Rather, it is evaluated alongside all of the other qualities in the selection team's search for leadership *potential*.

Think about some of the leaders throughout history and how they built their movements. Martin Luther King, Jr., perhaps the greatest leader of the 20th century, did not simply tell people to join him in Washington, D.C., on August 28, 1963. He inspired them through his words and his actions, so they decided to come to hear him speak. He became the voice and face of the civil rights movement because of his ability to lead people to a common vision. Barack Obama became president in 2008 because he helped the people of the United States believe in his ability to build a stronger nation. Voters of all ages, economic backgrounds, and races believed in his vision to enact change for a better America. These two figures, although different in their goals and aspirations, became leaders because they inspired people to join their respective movements and adopt their visions.

Leadership does not mean telling or forcing people to obey a command. A true leader convinces people that his path is the best one and helps them internalize his vision to make it their own. When you are in a classroom, you will be charged with leading your students to success. It is not enough to tell students that they must get good grades. Students must develop the inner desire to succeed, and believe they can succeed, or they will never achieve to their full potential. They need to internalize this desire, and it is the teacher's job to foster and facilitate that development. Teach For America wants to know that you have the potential to be that leader in the classroom.

Interpersonal Skills

To be a successful leader, you must be able to effectively communicate your message and vision. Your days will be spent talking and explaining concepts to students, planning with other teachers, and meeting with administrators. You will have to clearly explain your vision to the students and model it through your actions, so that they choose to internalize your goals. In fact, if you cannot communicate with others in an exceptionally strong way, then you probably won't be a good teacher (and chances are you won't like teaching very much either).

Interpersonal skills and personality are actually two very distinct concepts, although they are often confused with one another. Personality is the assortment of particular characteristics that both define a person and differentiate him from another. Interpersonal skills determine how an individual interacts with others. While personality reflects the internal constitution of a person, interpersonal skills are fundamentally external. A person can have an excellent personality but be unable to effectively work with and lead others. A person can have a boring personality but shine when placed with others in a professional environment. Of course, these are not mutually exclusive; many people with great personalities are also great communicators.

Teach For America does not look at your personality. In fact, the organization has determined that personality has no correlation with success as a teacher. What matters is that you have a superior ability to communicate with a wide range of people in a professional environment and lead them in a meaningful way. You need to be able to motivate a six-year-old student to read with the same conviction that you would need to lead a principal to adopt a school-wide management system.

Exhibiting These Qualities

Your ability to lead and your interpersonal skills are judged in many different parts of the application process. The selection team looks at your past achievements and involvements and analyzes the roles you took in those endeavors to determine your leadership potential. It really is not enough to simply involve yourself with impressive groups or organizations; you must take on decision-making and managing roles. Teach For America wants to see that you have been the team leader on a project, in a leadership position with an honors society, or featured in a newsletter about your major. The selection team wants to see that your role in the project led to a high grade, that you recruited a new set of members to your organization, or that the article written about you generated publicity on a controversial topic.

Experience leading groups of people will help to convince the selection team that you can successfully motivate others. Find these types of opportunities by talking to your professors or department advisors, and use them to your full advantage.

When applying and interviewing, take any chance you have to give examples of your ability to communicate with and motivate others. You should try to weave stories of teamwork and leadership into your letter of intent and responses to your interviewers whenever possible. If you are talking about a challenge you faced in your life, try to explain at least one specific way you communicated with other people to help work through that obstacle. The more you can show that you have effectively interacted with those you led, the better.

However, it is not enough to tell the readers and interviewers that you are a leader or that you interacted well with others; you have to convince them of these qualities during your actual interactions with them. Inspire the selection team to get behind you because of who you are, not because of what you tell them you have done. In writing your resume and letter of intent, recruit a lot of people to give you critical feedback on how they perceive your image and message. In preparing for the interviews, anticipate questions that will be asked of you and craft responses that flow logically and concisely. Practice talking about your resume and highlight your achievements with relevant quantitative results. Finally, as mentioned above, don't worry too much about letting your personality shine. The selection team does not have to like you per se. They have to be convinced that you can lead and motivate others to succeed.

Quality 3: Strong Achievement

Strong achievement in academic, professional, extracurricular, and/or volunteer settings

Strong leadership positions and quantifiable achievements in those roles can trump other inadequacies you might have in your application. Teach For America is in the business of results and success, and you must prove that you can deliver. The question, though, is how to best present your accomplishments in order to make the strongest impression possible on the selection team.

Ambitious, Quantifiable Results

The most effective way to present your achievements is by highlighting the ambitious, quantifiable results you obtained in those positions. To illustrate what I mean by "ambitious, quantifiable results," here are two possible ways the editor of a college newspaper could describe her position. Try to figure out which one does a better job of describing her achievements.

Response 1:

"As editor of XYZ University's newspaper, I was responsible for the news and editorial content of the paper and for setting all editorial and production deadlines. From the annual budget, I determined page budgets for the current issue and exercised final decision-making during disagreements between editors. My team increased the circulation of XYZ's newspaper by placing additional newsstands downtown."

Response 2:

"As editor of XYZ University's newspaper, I managed a team of 20 page editors, reporters, and photographers and assigned deadlines for each of their projects. I managed a yearly budget of $1.8

million and was charged with disbursing those funds to nine page editors on a quarterly basis. During my year as editor, my team increased the circulation of the newspaper from 20,000 readers to 33,000 readers by lobbying the City Council to allow XYZ to distribute newspapers downtown, away from campus, by placing 35 additional newspaper distributors on sidewalk corners, in local businesses, and in the downtown mall."

In the first response, the candidate speaks in broad terms about her role as editor. It is clear that she has a lot of responsibility, and it is impressive that circulation increased. However, we have very little sense of the degree and impact of her leadership or on the growth of the newspaper. Did she manage a staff of five or fifty people? Was her budget $5,000 or $5 million? By how much did the circulation increase? If she raised it by a couple of hundred readers, that might actually have fallen short of the newspaper's annual goal. But if she doubled the circulation in one year, that would be quite an accomplishment.

In the second version, the editor explains that she set the bar high for herself and showed true leadership in doing so. She includes the number of people she managed, the size of her budget, and how she expanded readership by lobbying her local government. We know exactly what she did, whom she led in the process, and how much money she had to do it. I'm impressed.

Exhibiting This Quality

Now, perhaps you are not the editor of your school paper. Only one person can have that position at a time (and if you are that person, congratulations!). At many schools, 10 percent or more of the graduating class applies to Teach For America. Let's look at how you can present your accomplishments in each of the listed categories: academic, professional, extracurricular, and volunteer.

Academic

There is no doubt that your GPA is important. The average GPA of Teach For America corps members is 3.6 on a 4.0 scale. Keep your GPA as high as possible and strive for straight As for the remainder of your time in college. Improvements are noticed, so if you began your college career with a low GPA, keep working at it. GPA is a measurable number that shows your level of achievement over a relatively long period of time. Do not underestimate it.

Your GPA, however, is not the only measure of your academic success. You may have some very substantial academic accomplishments or awards that are not reflected in your grades. Maybe you wrote an honors thesis that won the award for top thesis in your major. Talk about that success, the specific criteria and reasons why you won the award, and how many others were vying for the honor. Maybe a story you wrote for a creative writing class was submitted to a popular magazine by your professor and subsequently published. Explain that process and any benefits you received from it. Spend some time brainstorming other academic successes you have that don't show up in your GPA.

Professional

Many of you are applying to the corps having already pursued a different career. You may have managed a large staff, rallied colleagues on a project, or led community outreach efforts. You may have started your own successful business. If you are applying as an experienced professional, you likely have a whole lot to offer in terms of leadership experience, and you should quantify these successes in a truly meaningful way.

If you are still in college, you have likely worked at some point, whether part-time for a little extra spending money, during the summer as a paid (or unpaid) intern, or full-time to pay your tuition. Working full-time during college takes real leadership and responsibility, and if it applies to you, highlight it in your application. Paying your own way through college shows a commitment that is difficult to match in any other way.

Whether you have worked full-time for a decade or part-time during college, you hopefully were able to gain a position that allowed you to manage people and/or money, or to use your skills and ideas to influence the company's operations. While some jobs are inherently more impressive than others, there is opportunity for strong achievement in almost any situation. The manner in which you present that in your application and to your interviewer is essential; again, focus on the quantifiable outcomes you obtained.

Here are some ways to measure achievement in a few common college jobs. While certainly not exhaustive, these examples should give you a sense of how to think about your own professional experience (including if you have extensive post-graduate work experience).

1. **Resident Advisor:** How many students were on your floor? What specific resources did you provide to the students on your floor? Did you organize any memorable activities that brought your residents together? Did you have a budget to work with? Were you involved in the management or planning of the residence hall as a whole?

2. **Bank Teller:** Were you ever promoted to a position where you managed other employees or customers' accounts? If so, how many employees or accounts did you manage? Were you ever given a raise based on your performance? Were you ever asked to take on special projects that were outside the usual realm of a bank teller? Were you ever named Employee of the Week/Month/Year?

3. **Tutor:** Did you work for a tutoring company or set up your own client list? If you worked for a company, did you ever train other tutors or take a lead position? If you set up your own client list, how many clients did you have and what did you charge? How exactly did you find clients? What were the general outcomes of those you tutored (e.g., did they increase their grades by an average of one letter grade)?

4. **Restaurant Server:** Were you ever promoted to lead server, or did you have any responsibility for managing other servers or bussers? How much money did you handle per shift? How many customers did you wait on per shift? Did you take on any additional responsibilities outside the general realm of a server? Did you ever talk to the managers or owner about key decisions in the operations of the restaurant or sit in on budget meetings?

Extracurricular

Most of Teach For America's corps members were involved in extracurricular activities and organizations to some degree. The most common are honors societies (66 percent of corps members), faith-based organizations (45 percent), and the Greek system (34 percent). Many people were involved in diversity organizations, ski clubs, recreational sports, adventure clubs, arts communities, and service groups.

Think about your achievements in these organizations and the leadership positions you assumed, even informally, and quantify your results. If you were the philanthropy chair in your fraternity, how much money did you raise? What causes did you support and how many events did you organize? If you were in Hillel, did you lead an outreach campaign on campus? How many people did you reach? If you were in the adventure club, did you help recruit people to go on a weekend hiking trip? Did these people stay involved in the group after the trip ended?

Volunteer

When I talk to people about their chances of getting into Teach For America, they often say: "Jake, I've been volunteering as a tutor at a local school for a year now. I have experience teaching students, so why wouldn't they let me in?" Fifty-nine percent of corps members were involved in service of some kind during college, so volunteering in and of itself will not set you apart. What *will* set you apart is…get ready… *impressive achievements and the leadership roles you took on.*

If you went to an elementary school once per week and tutored fourth graders in a local school, you certainly helped students learn to read. If you worked directly with a professor and a teacher in the school to implement a new management system for the class—now that's impressive! If you worked with Big Brothers Big Sisters as a mentor for a few years and met your mentee once a month, you made a difference in a young man or woman's life. If you organized a trip for ten Big Brothers and Littles to go to Disneyland, and raised the funds to do it, you will stand apart from the other applicants.

If opportunities do not readily exist in your organization, create your own. If you see an opportunity to fulfill the organization's mission in a new and different way, put together a plan and present it to your superiors. You may get some resistance at first; even well-intentioned organizations are often scared of thinking outside the box. But if it is something you believe will really make a difference, use your leadership skills to make it happen. Planning it out well and assuming responsibility will make it easier for your boss to say yes. You will most likely give someone less fortunate a unique opportunity and gain real experience in what it means to create and lead.

My challenge to you is to take a more meaningful role in your academic, professional, extracurricular, and volunteer involvements. The other candidates have done many of the great things you have, but many have not taken their roles to the next level. Break out of your comfort zone and become a leader, and impressive accomplishments will follow.

Quality 4: Perseverance

Perseverance in the face of challenges, ability to adapt to changing environments, and a strong desire to do whatever it takes to improve and develop

"Perseverance" and "ability to adapt" are two separate skill sets, and the way you use them together is more of an art than a science. When you face inevitable challenges in the pursuit of your vision for the kids, you must persist through them and alter your path if need be. You are entering an industry in which you have no relevant experience, so you will most certainly struggle. It takes constant improvement to ensure that you can effectively navigate through challenges in new environments.

Perseverance in the Face of Challenges

To be sure, your work as a teacher will be challenging. While some of the obstacles you face will be one-time problems that you can solve immediately, most will be systematic issues that you will have to work both against and within in order to educate your students.

Perseverance is a more tedious quality than relentlessness. It is the essence of "sticking it out for the long haul." You will have to keep pushing closer and closer to your ultimate goal, regardless of what obstacles— including disruptive students and uncooperative coworkers—get in the way. You cannot let frustration or burnout get to you, and you certainly cannot give up.

To look at how important this quality is, let me introduce you to Dave. Dave works in sales for a commercial real estate firm. His team worked for two years just to get a meeting with the CEO of a major corporation. They left messages on his voicemail, with his secretary, and on his cell phone. They sent him financial projections and sample portfolios. They sent him gift baskets and sent his wife flowers on Mother's Day. Eighteen months later, they finally got a response, and six months after that, they got a meeting. At the meeting, the CEO asked Dave's team why he should partner with them. Dave responded, "Do you see how persistent we have been with you for two years? That is exactly how we will work for you every single day." This CEO is now a client.

Ability to Adapt to Changing Environments

If you are accepted into Teach For America, expect the unexpected. Things change quickly and often seemingly without reason. There will be times when you absolutely must change course, as the current path is just no longer feasible. However, adapting to changing environments does not mean giving up on your goals. It means having the determination and skill to alter your path to reach the same destination. If your goal is to create a welcoming environment in your classroom and three months into the school year your class absorbs ten new students, you should not lower your expectations for your classroom environment. You just have to instill the same principles in the new students as you have already begun doing with the original ones.

For a real-life example of this quality, let's look at Michael Phelps, the most decorated Olympian in history. Phelps's goal was always to win every race. His coach knew that there would be times when his environment would unexpectedly change, so he put obstacles in Phelps's way to teach him to adapt to unforeseen challenges. One of these obstacles was stepping on his goggles before a race started without his knowing, so that when Phelps dove into the pool, his goggles would fill up with water. Phelps was forced to adapt to these types of obstacles, and it paid off. During the 200-meter butterfly in the 2008 Olympics, his goggles suddenly filled up with water. Despite not being able to see for the last 100 meters,[2] he still won gold, clinching his tenth gold medal and becoming the all-time leader in gold medals won by an individual.

Continuous Improvement

In school, pure intelligence can take someone far, even with relatively minimal work. An incredibly bright student can slide by with a B average in college without fully applying himself. That simply does not hold true in teaching. Intelligence is an important quality to have, but only in the sense that a smart teacher can see trends more quickly, analyze data more effectively, and understand content better.

As in any difficult endeavor, there is a learning curve that you will have to overcome. The actual practice of teaching is a craft that takes a lot of time and energy to learn, and you will be starting from square one. You must continually improve and develop your craft throughout your time in the corps to become an exemplary teacher. If you are not willing to put in the energy it takes to improve, you will quickly burn out and fall short of your goals. Just like playing sports or creating art, learning to be an effective teacher is an ongoing process at which you can always improve.

Exhibiting These Qualities

We all have faced challenges in our lives at one time or another. We have overcome difficulties and grown from those challenges in a positive way. However, chances are that, unless you have already taught in a low-income school, you have never quite faced the kinds of obstacles you will face daily as a corps member. Again, Teach For America knows this. What you need to show the selection team is how you took on a challenge, persevered, and learned from the experience.

When thinking through difficult situations you have faced, start to brainstorm how you would answer interview questions about these challenges. Be ready to speak directly about the situation, what you did in spite of the obstacles, and what happened in the end. Making the challenges and outcomes quantifiable will make your story even stronger.

---

2 Phelps, Michael. 2008. *No Limits: The Will to Succeed.* New York: Free Press.

Think about some of the difficult situations you have faced in your life. For each one, you should answer these three questions:

1. What was the challenge that you faced?

2. What did you do to work through it?

3. What was the outcome?

Many of us have gone through difficult personal obstacles in our lives. You can discuss these hurdles if you are comfortable talking about them. Maybe you lost a close family member at a young age and were left to take care of a sibling. How did you persevere through that difficult time in your life so that you could still pursue your goals? Were you able to rise to the occasion and accept the additional responsibility? Maybe you moved six times during high school because of your mom's job. How did you stay focused on maintaining your grades, and how did you manage the mental strain?

In addition to personal obstacles, you can also revisit academic, professional, volunteer, and extracurricular activities from the previous section. What kinds of challenges did you face in order to succeed in those experiences?

Academic

If you wrote a long honors thesis, how did you sustain the energy to write a hundred-page paper? Did you consult others to help you through it, budget time every day to work on it, or see your advisor on a weekly basis? Did you organize focus groups or conduct wide-reaching surveys? Did you run into any unforeseen obstacles, like a computer crashing or a study being released that refuted your argument? Did you do anything extraordinary to improve your thesis that no one else did? Did you achieve anything remarkable as a result of writing it?

Professional

If you were given an especially complex project that you had to finish quickly in a summer job, how did you stay focused throughout the project and what did you do when things went wrong? How did you react to criticism and your boss's pressuring you for results? Did your boss ever change his expectations for the project? If so, how did you ensure that you still met your goal? Did you take classes outside of work to improve your ability to perform the tasks required of you? Was your boss ultimately satisfied with the outcome? What kind of feedback did you receive?

Volunteer/Extracurricular

If you volunteered as a Big Brother in Big Brothers Big Sisters, did you ever receive harsh criticism from a parent? How did you mitigate that conflict? Did you ultimately lead the parent to see the benefits of the relationship, or did he feel ostracized? Were you able to figure out a deeper reason for the criticism? Did something devastating happen to your Little that made the child's goals more difficult to achieve? If your background was different from his, did you do anything out of the ordinary to understand his perspective a little better?

Quality 5: Critical Thinking

Excellent critical thinking skills, including the ability to accurately link cause and effect and to generate relevant solutions to problems

Teachers are always engaged in critical thinking. Things happen in a classroom, both good and bad, and it is the responsibility of the teacher to discover why they are happening. If students exhibit positive behavior or academic success, it is imperative to know why and ensure that progress continues. If students are struggling, it is equally important to find the cause of the problem and then solve it.

Teachers are forced to think critically in two different ways. The first is analyzing why certain things are occurring over a relatively long period of time and ensuring that positive events continue and negative ones are fixed. The second is reacting to events as they occur immediately, or in real time. The first requires deep reflection on methodology and diligent implementation of new strategies. The second requires strong anticipation of classroom dynamics and quick reaction to problems. The good news is that you will improve in both of these areas over time, especially if you work hard at them, but you should still try to develop these skills ahead of time to some degree.

Long-Term

When working on a problem that is happening over a period of time, effective teachers address the cause of the problem instead of the problem itself. Chances are that a reasonable explanation can be located and identified. Finding the root cause of a problem is a process that takes deep reflection and forces teachers to make connections to arrive at the underlying issue.

Let's take one simple example that you will likely see countless times as a Teach For America corps member:

"Why does John come to class late every day?"

Although it may appear on the surface that John simply does not care about his grades, there are many reasons why tardiness occurs. Sometimes the reasons are direct: He has to drop off his sister at her elementary school, his previous teacher has a habit of keeping students late to clean up the classroom, or he has problems with another student and is taking a longer way to class to avoid confrontation. It is easy to find a solution to these causes. Advising him to leave the house earlier to drop off his sister, explaining to his other teacher the importance of letting John out on time, or talking to a counselor about the problem with the other student are all actions a teacher can and should take.

Often, however, the problem lies deeper within the teacher's own classroom. John may simply not understand the connection between coming to class on time and his learning potential. It sounds intuitive, but many students have never been taught the short-term and long-term effects of tardiness. If this is the case, the teacher needs to clearly demonstrate why it is essential to come to class on time. It may take days, weeks, or months for John to internalize the connection, but understanding the reason will get him on his way to success. Discovering the root problem and leading John to fully digest the connection are not easy to do, but they are essential skills of a great teacher.

In Real Time

Sometimes, teachers have to link cause with effect immediately and react in the most appropriate and effective way. This often happens when a student acts inappropriately or their classroom is disrupted in some way. Katherine just angrily walked out of class. What should I do? Carlos's cell phone just went off for the second time this period. How do I handle this situation? A mouse just ran across the floor of my classroom, and everyone started screaming. How do I get the class back on task?

There will be times when a new teacher will react inappropriately in these situations, especially during the first few months of teaching. These moments can be incredibly stressful and emotionally taxing, and they are where incoming corps members tend to struggle the most. It is not fun when a student curses at you or a first grader runs rampant through your classroom. Fortunately, you will become better and better at dealing with these situations as you get more comfortable and experienced in the classroom.

Exhibiting This Quality

You will likely be asked in an interview to talk about a problem you faced and how you figured out how to solve it. You need to identify a few examples from your past experiences and be ready to speak about how you approached the situations. If you are not asked directly about your ability to think critically, sprinkle it in with your answers to other questions. For example, when discussing your leadership on a project, part of your answer could be: "...and that really forced me to think critically about why we were getting so many negative reactions. We looked at X, Y, and Z, and realized that by altering the wording of Y, we could completely change the image of our experiment. Then, reactions quickly turned positive."

In addition to the interview, your ability to think through problems and find solutions will be tested in the form of a short online activity (which we'll look at more in Chapter 8). In addition to other problems, you will be required to analyze a set of data and come to a conclusion about what the data reveal.

Quality 6: Planning and Managing Responsibilities

Superior organizational ability, including planning well and managing responsibilities effectively

These are actually two different skill sets. The ability to plan in a detailed and effective way is very different from making sure you are completing all of your tasks on time. Once again, let's break this down into sections.

Planning Well

On your first day at Teach For America's summer Institute, your instructors will start talking to you about backward planning. In backward planning, you start with what you want your students to know *at the end* of the lesson/week/unit/year and then plan back to the beginning in meticulous detail to ensure that you get there. This method is very effective for keeping your plan focused on the skill or concept you are teaching and making sure it flows logically. You very well may have never planned anything with as much diligence as you will plan every lesson, unit, and year-long goal as a teacher.

The process of backward planning is mapped out below:

Setting the end goal: What do I want to accomplish at the end of the project? What does it mean to accomplish that goal?

Measuring the end goal: How will I know that I have accomplished that goal? What does success actually look like?

Outlining the plan: How will I get to that goal? What are the steps, in order, that need to happen to succeed?

Planning each step: What kinds of actions do I need to take to accomplish each of those steps?

Backward planning is not limited to teaching. It is a universal approach for achieving goals, both personal and professional, because it forces you to stay focused on the path to your destination. To put it in context, here are two very different examples of backward planning in situations completely unrelated to teaching.

Dating

Normal planning: You hang out at bars, parties, and art openings, hoping to find a girl you like. You are not quite sure what qualities you are seeking. You go out to dinner with a lot of different girls who have a lot of different qualities. Some are too standoffish, some are too aggressive, and some have dull personalities. Finally, you find an outgoing girl who played volleyball in college and likes to play in recreation leagues. After a year of dating, you realize that she just isn't a nice person and break it off. You loved playing sports with her, but now you realize how important it is to be with someone who is "nice," although you're not exactly sure what that means. Thus, you are back to square one.

Backward planning: You reflect on your past relationships and realize that you want to find a girl who is both nice and athletic. Your next step is to figure out what each of those traits means. What qualities do you classify as nice, and what qualities do you classify as athletic? You decide that the way a girl demonstrates "niceness" is by volunteering, and the way she shows "athleticism" is by actively playing sports. Now, you need to start planning for how to find this girl. You decide to get involved with a nonprofit that organizes soccer leagues for inner-city children. Chances are, your new girlfriend is just waiting for you to arrive at the next tournament.

Launching a New Product

Normal planning: You have developed a new software product that makes it easy to hold meetings over the Internet and allows participants to share and edit documents in real time. You have finished creating the product and set your price.

You contact the CEOs of a hundred companies, requesting a meeting to present your new software system. Two of the CEOs agree to meet with you, but when you deliver your presentation, they tell you they are unwilling to take the risk of purchasing your software because it is untested and more expensive than their current systems. You decide to cut the price of the product in half and spend the following months re-launching the product to a different set of CEOs.

Backward planning: You determine that your goal is to have 60 companies beta-testing your product by the end of the first year, and have 75 percent of those companies sign up for the full service by the end of the second year. You will know if you have accomplished that goal by measuring how many companies are in beta-testing and how many of them sign up for the full service. To achieve that goal, you recognize that you need to provide incentives for the companies to beta-test your product, so you offer the beta period for free. In addition, if they decide to buy the software at the end of the testing period, they will receive three months of free service. During the beta period, you plan biweekly check-ins with each company to work out any bugs, and you have a short but comprehensive survey sent out each month to gauge satisfaction. You schedule ten focus groups at strategic times throughout the year for the main users of the software to brainstorm solutions and price points. At the end of the year, you launch an improved version 2.0 of the product and offer an additional month of free service for each company the original companies refer to you.

At its core, planning backward keeps you on task and allows you to anticipate potential obstacles. By defining the end goal in an easily measurable way, you force yourself to develop concrete steps to reach that goal. When I discuss designing your five-minute lesson for the final interview in Chapter 11, you will have an opportunity to actually go through a backward-planning process, with step-by-step guides and worksheets to help you develop your lesson plan.

Exhibiting This Quality

If you have never planned at this level or in this manner, how do you demonstrate that you can do it? In actuality, you probably have done this already to some extent without realizing it. If you planned a philanthropy event for your sorority, you had to establish a fundraising goal. How did you set that goal, and what did you do to make sure you reached it? If you wrote an honors thesis for graduation, your goal probably included both length and grade. How did you plan your time to get there? You can use this framework for nearly any project that you have planned or helped to plan.

Try sitting down and mapping out one of these more complex projects and really delve into the kind of thinking you went through, even if you did not structure it as such at the time. My guess is that you will surprise yourself with how much you planned backward from a desired end result, especially if you reached your goal. Even if you don't find evidence of backward planning, try implementing it in an upcoming project. This could be anything from writing a five-page essay for your writing class to creating a new file system at work. It will pay off to learn to approach projects in this way, whether or not you end up as a teacher.

Managing Responsibilities Effectively

Deciding how and when to complete your responsibilities is a much different task than planning. On any given day as a teacher, you may have 10–15 important tasks to accomplish. Some of the tasks will need to be done that afternoon; others will have no set deadline. You will have to decide how to manage them so that you can complete them all. Your "to do" list for any given time, in no specific order of importance, may look something like this:

- Write next week's lesson plans and submit them to the principal (5 hours)

- Create "station" activity for English tomorrow (1 hour)

- Grade essays turned in last week (4 hours)

- Create homework handout for tomorrow (30 minutes)

- Call parents of Jordan, Carlos, Anthony, Alex, and Catherine to let them know that their children received As on the most recent test (3–7 minutes per call)

- Create interim reports for all students to send home next Monday (3 hours)

- Take down old student work from walls and hang up new student work (1 hour)

- Organize classroom library (30 minutes)

- Make note of any students with poor attendance over the past two weeks (45 minutes)

- Create new behavior management system for seventh-period class (3 hours)

- Read *To Kill a Mockingbird* to prepare for next month's unit (~12 hours)

Everything on this list is important. Some of these tasks have steadfast deadlines. For example, you will not be able to teach your class tomorrow if you don't prepare activities. Others are very time-sensitive. Calling your students' parents with positive news becomes less and less of a reward the longer you wait. Many more have open-ended deadlines or no deadline at all. No one is telling you when to replace student work or create a new behavior management system.

Add in the fact that you most likely will be attending graduate school and that you will have additional responsibilities with Teach For America, and you may have half a dozen other obligations that have no direct relationship with your job as a teacher. It can easily become overwhelming and difficult to balance. The number of hours in your day is limited, and you must show Teach For America that you do not get overwhelmed when juggling dozens of these types of responsibilities.

Exhibiting This Quality

My biggest piece of advice is to keep a calendar, if you don't do so already. This is not just useful for Teach For America; having a detailed calendar where you can mark off completed assignments, rank tasks according to importance, and move around entries can do wonders for your productivity. Google Calendar is a tremendous example of a free resource with almost unlimited capabilities to this end. During the interviews, you should be able to talk in detail about the system you use to stay on task and manage your responsibilities. If you use a form of "organized chaos" or have three separate calendars that you use in conjunction with each other, that's fine. Just make sure you can explain the system to someone else in a concise way.

There are many ways to prioritize responsibilities. You can use a number system, where a "1" signifies something that is extremely urgent and a "5" is something that can wait indefinitely (you can also use a color system in the same way if you are more of a visual person). You can create separate lists for tasks with steadfast deadlines and those with more open-ended ones, and then prioritize within those lists. You can draw arrows to move uncompleted tasks to the following day, and write next to them how many days they have gone uncompleted. None of these methods work for everyone, but pick a few and try them out with your current responsibilities. Over time, you will develop a method that allows you to effectively manage your to-do list.

As a side note, one question you will likely be asked by an interviewer is if you have ever missed a deadline. The answer is almost certainly, "Yes." The key to answering this question well is to acknowledge a time you missed a deadline, talk about the reasons that led to missing it (without making excuses), and then discuss how you remedied the situation and lessons you took away from the experience. You should pick a time that had specific, measurable consequences and then talk about how you worked through the missed deadline to get back on track. Most importantly, explain the steps that you have taken since to ensure that you never miss a similar deadline again.

Quality 7: Respect for All Backgrounds

Respect for individuals' diverse experiences and the ability to work effectively with people from a variety of backgrounds

Your students may be of different races or socioeconomic levels than you. It is crucial not only to respect your students, but also to be willing to work diligently alongside them. You must be able to respect a person and her ideas according to who she is as an individual, not the color of her skin or her income level. Intuitively you know this, or you would not be applying to Teach For America, but if you are not used to working in a diverse setting, this can be harder in practice than it seems.

It is, of course, not only the students who differ from you in their experiences and backgrounds. You must be able to respect and work with *everyone* around you, no matter their backgrounds, experiences, ideologies, races, or income levels. Notice how Teach For America does not limit this quality to "respect for other races" or "respect for low-income students." There will be times when your ideologies will come into conflict with the experiences and backgrounds of coworkers, administrators, parents, or community leaders. You may have a principal who is heavily invested in your school district's politics and fellow teachers who are big supporters of policies with which you do not agree. Instead of judging your peers, try to put yourself in their shoes and see things from their perspective. If you can do this, you will be better suited to present an argument that they can internalize and lead them to at least consider your opinion.

Well before you step into the classroom for the first time, you will be interacting and working with people of diverse backgrounds and experiences. During Institute, you will be placed on a team with three incoming corps members with whom you will spend countless hours planning, strategizing, and teaching. You all will enter Teach For America with your own biases and ideas of what to do in the classroom. You must prove that you can effectively work with a wide range of people and personalities. Remember that being a leader does not mean telling people that your way is correct; being a leader means helping people buy into your vision so that they choose to come to your side.

Exhibiting This Quality

It can be difficult to convey "respect" in an interview. Obviously you would never tell an interviewer that you don't respect people of different backgrounds. Rather, this quality is best represented by always acting and speaking professionally. Interviewers and essay readers will notice if you inadvertently slip and show a bias against a certain group. They are watching how you respond to questions about the people you will work with and teach during your two years.

When speaking about students, you should always use student-friendly language, showing the utmost respect for the children you will be charged with educating. From my experience, however, applicants more often make the mistake of disrespecting coworkers, parents, and school districts in interviews, rather than students themselves. If you have, for example, a strong bias for or against teachers' unions, leave it out of your responses. This is not the time to speak disrespectfully, even "off the cuff," about other groups. If the subject does come up, it is important to craft your answer in a way that both demonstrates your point and conveys respect. This is especially important to keep in mind during the discussion exercise in the final interview.

To illustrate how to answer difficult questions in a respectful manner, here are two different responses to a question on education policy. While your interviewer will likely not ask a question this directly about a controversial topic, the goal here is to demonstrate how to speak respectfully, while still getting your message across. Let's call the interviewee Chris.

Question: What is your opinion on tenure in public schools?

Answer 1: In my opinion, the education gap can be largely attributed to teachers who are so protected by tenure that they no longer have any incentive to do their jobs. They simply watch the days move by and collect a paycheck every couple of weeks, without so much as trying to teach their students. The biggest problem is that the idiotic administrations and school district policies just pass these kids on through the system. By high school, they are so far behind that even energetic teachers are unable to reverse the damage. Yes, there may be some strong teachers who have been justly protected from bad administrations, but for the most part, tenure is a huge problem.

As you undoubtedly noted, this answer is loaded with red flags. Chris uses blanket, biased generalizations to form opinions, suggesting that he may have difficulty working with others. He categorizes teachers as lazy, without so much as attempting to get the full picture. His use of the word "idiotic" is the clear opposite of being respectful. A little more subtle, but equally disrespectful, is the tone with which Chris talks about students in a manner that is not student-friendly. The unfortunate situation of kids being multiple grade levels behind in high school comes from a wide range of factors. If Chris was talking about a student in my class, I would be quick to inform him that my students are not "damaged." In all, this answer is probably enough to lead the selection team to drop Chris's application into the "rejected" pile.

Let's see if we can get the same overall message across—that tenure in its current form is a negative policy—while maintaining respect for others.

> **Answer 2:** The issue of tenure in schools is an incredibly complicated issue. On one hand, it is a way for unions to exercise their rights against administrations and school districts that may unfairly fire a teacher for petty reasons. On the other hand, I fear that it has too often protected teachers who want to take advantage of the system. There is no doubt that strong teachers need to have a structure in place to protect them, but I think we need to implement accountability measures in the process so that our students are not "handcuffed" to ineffective teachers.

Is Chris still voicing his opinion? Absolutely. Would he still elicit a harsh response from a strong supporter of tenure? You bet he would. But Chris is not offending anyone with his argument. He is acknowledging that tenure is complicated and that there are teachers who fall on both sides of the issue. He presents an alternative to the current system and justifies it by discussing how it benefits students. While he challenges the teachers who are not living up to expectations, he is not generalizing tenured teachers as a whole.

Working with Diverse Backgrounds: My Story

When I joined Teach For America, I was quickly introduced to the need to have the utmost respect not only for students, but also for coworkers.

I taught special education in a large, comprehensive public high school during my two years in the corps. All of the teachers come in to school a week before students arrive to pick up official rosters, set up classrooms, and meet with the administration and content teams. At the end of the first day, I found out that I would be co-teaching Algebra II. I went to our assigned classroom to see if the other teacher would show up. No one came.

I arrived the next day and went up to my classroom to wait. Five minutes later, a woman walked in and asked who I was. I introduced myself and told her I was her co-teacher for the year. She was a bit older than me and had a strong Eastern-European accent. Needless to say, she wasn't too thrilled about the idea. She said that there must be some mistake and that she didn't need a co-teacher. I didn't know what to say.

We spent the next several days talking and getting to know each other. She had come to the United States from Albania eight years earlier, knowing almost no English. She learned English by substitute teaching and talking to students during class. She loved kids and constantly worked to become a better teacher.

We had different ideas of how to teach the class, starting from day one. I wanted to spend the first week developing class goals and helping students buy into the class. She thought that this would waste valuable instructional time and wanted to start with chapter one immediately. We argued about this during that whole first week.

As a new teacher, I decided to defer to her. She was experienced—she had taught for eight years—so I stepped back to learn from her. I learned a lot during those first few weeks, but I also began to see ways I thought would make our class more effective, so I brought them up. Sometimes she agreed with me, other times she resisted. I countered with my own arguments, and conversations started. We were still getting to know each other, and still learning to trust one another. This was the beginning of one of the most rewarding team relationships I have ever experienced. In our two years of teaching together, I think I spent more time with her than her husband did.

We worked through our differences. As the weeks went on, we would discuss our strategies for our classes daily, and pretty quickly we started listening more and more to each other's ideas. We implemented the ones that were obviously strong and threw out the ones that were obviously flawed. We felt comfortable discussing and debating the rest of them to ensure that our class would be as strong as possible. We figured out each other's strengths and weaknesses, and segmented our duties in the classroom to match them. Throughout the two years, we had many heated debates to the point of screaming, but also times when we laughed ourselves to tears. At the heart of it, we both grew to respect each other immensely and knew that we both wanted what was best for our kids.

Once you can put yourself in other people's shoes and assume they want what they believe is best based on their experiences, it is much easier to respect their opinions and work out a solution that suits everyone. This can take some time—it took months before my co-teacher and I were at that level—but it is important to have the utmost respect for those with whom you interact and continue to work to make the relationships stronger.

—Jake Whitman (Philadelphia '09)

Summary

You should spend a lot of time thinking about how to convey these seven core competencies using your unique background. You should also think about how you measure up against them to gauge your fit for the organization. Teach For America has spent a lot of time, energy, and money identifying and developing these qualities, and the program uses them consistently nationwide to select its corps.

All seven of these qualities are inherently laced together. When you succeed in leading a diverse group of people to a lofty goal, you do so by believing strongly in the vision, communicating that vision well, planning efficiently and thinking critically about the plan, persevering through obstacles, respecting those around you, and, when necessary, being relentless. In your application and interviews, when discussing your experiences, your personal goals, and your understanding of Teach For America, these seven qualities should shine through.

Chapter 4

Set Yourself Apart

There are a number of experiences and skills you can gain that will exemplify Teach For America's seven core competencies outlined in the previous chapter. In building these faculties, the earlier you start reading this book, the better. If you are a freshman, sophomore, or junior, you have a lot of opportunity to capitalize on your time in college to develop these skills. If you are a senior and applying now, I encourage you to act on these suggestions during your senior year, even after you apply and get accepted. They will help ease the transition into teaching and make you become a better teacher faster. Getting accepted is just the tip of the iceberg—you will soon have a class of anxious, eager, talented, and sometimes unruly children to teach.

If you really push yourself to build these skills and experiences, you will have more meaningful achievements to reference in your letter of intent and interviews. You will demonstrate that you took the initiative to develop these skills while still in college, which shows dedication and persistence. Do not be scared to do something with the purpose of learning how to struggle outside of your comfort zone. That's what college is for, and taking advantage of that opportunity shows confidence and resilience.

In writing this chapter, I thought long and hard about the most important experiences and skills an applicant and corps member can have, but I realized that I have only a limited perspective from my personal experiences. I thought it would be exponentially more beneficial to enlist the help of dozens of corps members, alumni, and staff members to assist me in determining what is most important. To get their opinions, I asked each of them two simple questions:

1. What is the most important skill or mindset you think incoming corps members should possess to be successful?

2. What is the one thing you think corps members could do in college to help themselves build that skill before they enter Teach For America?

When reading their answers, I quickly noticed that certain recommendations kept recurring, showing that there really are concrete steps you can take to better prepare yourself for the application now and the profession further on. In this chapter, I lay out the five most prevalent skills and experiences that will help you prepare for both the application process and the classroom. Following these recommendations will make you stand out from other applicants and impress the application readers and interviewers.

For each recommendation, I first define the skill or experience and then present ways you can develop it by taking action right now. I am also including verbatim a number of responses I received from corps members and alumni that express the importance of that skill or experience, so you can hear directly from the people who do this work every day.

Recommendation 1: Learn How to Fail

The absolute number one response I received was to learn how to fail at something, fail often, and then work to overcome that failure. In your efforts to educate your students to the highest degree possible, you will face constant obstacles and difficulties. Inevitably, if you are accepted into Teach For America, you will not only fail early and often, you will fail *hard*. You will fail in emotionally devastating ways that can be quite difficult to overcome (which is where resilience and perseverance come in).

At some point, you may work for a month on a lesson unit and have all but one of your students fail the test. You will then have to spend an entire two weeks re-teaching the unit. This is time that you do not have to spare, and your students may complain that they are bored by the content. At times, you will feel that you let your students down, and at times it will seem impossible to change course. You will pray at night that you get into a car crash that doesn't quite kill you—just breaks a leg or two—so you won't have to face the kids the next day. (OK, maybe that's an exaggeration, but few corps members will deny that they think about unavoidable absences at least occasionally.)

People who get accepted into Teach For America are generally not people who are used to failure. Incoming corps members usually have degrees from prestigious colleges, very high GPAs, records as captains of sports teams or presidents of fraternities, and supreme confidence in their abilities.

The good thing is that the people Teach For America selects are also great at learning how to deal with and overcome failure, but it often takes some time. If you have never truly failed before, NOW is the time to learn. You need to put yourself in some difficult and uncomfortable situations to learn what it means to fail, and then not only get back up, but push even harder for success. You will not only feel more prepared when it happens for the first time in a classroom, but also fail less often when it matters most and know how to bounce back quickly and effectively when you do.

> "Applicants need to learn what it feels like to fail at something. While no one in college, especially those applying to TFA, strive to sign up for something where they will inevitably fail, I do feel it's important to step out of your comfort zone and put yourself in a situation where someone might say no to you, or you might not accomplish what you set out to do. The first and many subsequent times this failure happens during Institute and the two years have the potential to sting a lot, and having that 'tougher skin' before stepping into your school is key."
>
> —Sara '10
>
> "Put yourself in situations where you will struggle and hopefully experience some failure. There is never a surefire way to prepare yourself for difficult challenges or to know exactly how you will respond to them. However, prior to stepping foot in a classroom, you can take chances, try new things, and put yourself in an environment that pushes your skills—somewhere new, where success is not a given and failure will be a part the experience."
>
> —Alyson '02

And my personal favorite:

"Try things you have never done so you can become comfortable with sucking at something and grow confident in the belief that you can get better at something you suck at."
—Marina '09

How You Can Develop This Skill/Experience

You need to learn how to work tirelessly at something that you are passionate about. You have to fight through challenges, get back up again, and work even harder. You absolutely cannot give up; you must work relentlessly until you succeed.

Here are the steps to fail at something successfully:

1. Sign up for or commit to something challenging that is related to a passion of yours.

2. Make sure this "something" is very difficult.

3. Work as hard as you can to succeed at it.

4. When you inevitably struggle and then fail, DO NOT GIVE UP.

5. Keep working at it until you succeed, even if it takes you a lot longer than you imagined.

If you follow these steps, not only will you know what it's like to persist through something difficult, but you will also have achieved something that you care about deeply. You will also be able to tell your interviewer, "I've always been great at X but never really tried to apply it to what I'm passionate about. So, I decided to try [insert something difficult] while in college, even though I had never done anything like it before. Although it seemed nearly impossible at the time, I eventually succeeded, and I learned A, B, and C in the process." Teach For America loves to see its applicants pursue something that they are passionate about and overcome obstacles to achieve an ambitious goal.

Here are some concrete things you can do to learn how to fail and then overcome that failure. You will notice that each of the items on the list includes a measurement of success. The items vary widely, so some of these may be things you already do or think will not be so difficult. Others will be things that you think are next to impossible for you to achieve. However, there is nothing on this list that cannot be done.

When reading through this list, write "E" in the space next to the items you think will be easy, "M" next to the ones you think will be moderately difficult, "H" next to the ones you think will be hard, and "I" next to those you think would be impossible.

____1. If you love to travel, sign up to study the language spoken in your dream destination (as long as you don't already speak the language) and keep taking classes until you are able to have a general conversation in that language with your professor during office hours.

____2. If you love listening to music but are not musically talented, start taking music theory. The goal is to get an A in, at minimum, an intermediate music theory class.

____3. If education has always been your passion, sign up to be a teacher's assistant in a school for an entire year. Work with your teacher to set a meaningful goal for your class, such as 80 percent mastery of all math objectives or a reading growth of 1.5 times average growth, and make sure your students meet that goal.

____4. If you are great at physics, engineering, or even just math, enter into a robotics or similar competition and advance to the national level. If you do not make it on your first try, keep entering competitions until you do.

____5. If you are an art history major, but not an artist, sign up for an art class. Develop your skills until you are able to sell your drawing, painting, or photograph to someone you do not know.

____6. If you love sports or music, try contacting your favorite athlete or musician and do not stop trying until you get him or her on the phone. This can actually be easier than you think if you are confident and have a specific, relevant question in mind to ask.

___7. No matter what you are passionate about, do a live radio or television broadcast about that passion. Contact your college's radio station or TV channel and ask to be a guest on the show for a half-hour segment.

___8. If you enjoy theater but have never actually performed, try out for school plays and don't stop until you get a main role. (It doesn't have to be the lead role, but it never hurts to strive for the top!)

___9. Start a nonprofit organization on an issue you care deeply about or start a business in something you do well. Go through all of the legal processes of incorporating the company. Then, actually fulfill your organization's mission or make your business profitable.

___10. If you are athletic, run a marathon. You don't have to set a time goal for yourself unless you really want to. Running a marathon in and of itself is a remarkable goal.

Now, cross out the numbers you ranked as "E" and "M." Take a look at the ones you marked "I." Are they really *impossible* (i.e., you are a senior, and there are no more school plays this year) or just highly *improbable* (i.e., your favorite musician is Bono, and he seems untouchable)? For any that are just improbable, change them to "H." Then, from your list of original and new Hs, pick one that speaks to you and go for it, or think of something equally challenging to pursue. If you achieve your first one more quickly than you anticipated, congratulations! Now pick another one and try again.

There is nothing quite like succeeding at a seemingly impossible task that advances a cause that you are passionate about. The more you try, the better you will get at overcoming obstacles and pushing through small and large failures.

Recommendation 2: Understand and Work with Low-Income Students

Close behind experiencing failure is the need to work with low-income students and feel comfortable doing so. Unless you come from a low-income area (which you may), you really cannot understand how education operates in high-need schools. Even if you did attend school in a low-income community, you may still have some misconceptions because you were a student, not a teacher. I will go so far as to say that you cannot fully appreciate Teach For America's mission until you spend some time in a low-income school on the other side of the teacher's desk.

"The more experience you have working with students, the better prepared you will be to teach them. You need to GET kids. Understanding and liking kids is essential to motivating them and gaining their respect."

—Katy '09

"It would be great if TFAers could take a course during the spring of senior year that introduces them to the basics of teaching and helps them identify the mindset and skill gaps on which they need to work. It would be a huge benefit to start Institute having a better picture of who you are as a teacher and what you need to work on."

—Pat '09

"Work with the age group you will be teaching and have strong background knowledge into the complexities of poverty."

—Lauren '11

Now, I know I mentioned in Chapter 3 that simply working for an organization or tutoring students will not set you apart. I stand by that. You should continually work toward gaining more responsibility as you get more comfortable and skilled in your position. You may start out just tutoring students twice a week for an hour at a time. However, you should ask the teacher for more responsibility after a few weeks. Ask if you can lead part of a lesson, and then a couple weeks later ask to lead a full lesson. Solicit constructive feedback from the teacher and don't be offended when told you messed something up or need to change something. Then, try again.

How You Can Develop This Skill/Experience

The very first thing you should do is find out if Teach For America places teachers where you live or close to where you live. If it does, contact a member of the recruitment team at your university[1] or call the local Teach For America office and request to observe a teacher for a day. Tell the person who answers the phone your name, your college, your year in school, your interest in learning more about Teach For America and applying to the corps, and your request to observe a corps member for a day. From there, whoever answered the phone will likely either take down your information and get back to you or transfer you to another staff member who will talk to you a little bit more about your availability and your preference for grade level and/or subject. The great thing about this is, not only will you get to see a Teach For America teacher in action for a day and pick her brain about the program, you will be showing initiative and putting your name on the Teach For America radar.

If you are not in a Teach For America placement region, contact local schools at the grade level you want to teach and ask to observe a teacher for a day. Sometimes it can be harder to get schools to agree to this, so you might get rejected a few times before you find a willing school—but hey, that's good practice in being persistent.

Now, observing a teacher for a day is a great way to *see* the school and what you will do every day if accepted into Teach For America, but it will not give you extensive experience in working with students. To do that, you need to find a way to work with students or a teacher at least once a week for a few months. This can be harder to organize but is extremely important.

Here are some ways to get involved in working with students:

1　Email recruitment@teachforamerica.org and ask who the recruitment manager is at your school or in your region.

1. Talk to the education department at your college or university
    about the classes they offer or partnerships they have with local
    school districts or charter schools that would place you directly
    in a school. You should emphasize your preference for working in
    a low-income school instead of a high-income school, so you can
    experience that environment. They may assume you are looking to
    work in the best school possible, so make that point clear.

2. Research nonprofit organizations in your area that work with
    students in schools either during the day or after school. There
    are likely dozens of these types of organizations, and they are
    constantly looking for energetic volunteers to tutor students and
    help run programs. Some renowned national nonprofits to look
    into are City Year, YMCA, Boys and Girls Clubs of America, Big
    Brothers Big Sisters, Citizen Schools, Learn and Serve America,
    and Jumpstart for Young Children. There are likely also many
    other local nonprofits that work solely in your city or state,
    especially if you live in or close to an urban environment. Local
    nonprofits, as opposed to national ones, tend to be smaller,
    providing you with more opportunities to quickly gain a
    leadership position.

3. Contact charter schools in your area and ask about opportunities
    to tutor students either during or after school. Be honest with
    them about your qualifications and emphasize your interest in
    teaching and desire to work with students. Charters generally have
    more flexibility than public schools, so they may have programs
    in place that are staffed entirely by volunteers. If the first charter
    school you call does not have any openings, keep trying.

4. Contact local public schools and inquire about their tutoring
    opportunities. Depending on the size of the school district, they
    may have much more stringent policies than charter schools,
    but there is a lot of need in many of these schools, so your time
    will make a strong impact. Often, there will be local nonprofit
    organizations working in the school to which the administration
    can connect you. This is a great way to get in contact with
    nonprofits from option 2 above.

Whatever route you choose, you should find a way to work with students at some point in college. It will be rewarding, and you will quickly learn if it is right for you. If you have never tutored or worked with kids before, this is a great way to get comfortable in doing so (and probably fail a couple of times in the process). This does not have to be your primary volunteer or professional work while in college, but it will give you great perspective for Teach For America's application and interview process and demonstrate how you have put forth the effort to gain some meaningful experiences.

During my final quarter in college as a business economics major, after I had already been accepted to Teach For America, I took my first and only education class. We spent the majority of the class on-site at a local low-income elementary school, tutoring students in reading. I had not been inside an elementary school since leaving my own in 1999. I spent the first week watching and doing exactly as the teacher told me. Gradually, he turned responsibility over to me and would watch me as I tutored the students. After each half-hour session, I asked him to give me unrestrained feedback so I could get better. Halfway through the quarter, I was tutoring students completely on my own, allowing us to work with twice as many students. By the end of the 10-week quarter, I was working with other teachers in the school to maximize my time. I had already been accepted into Teach For America, but those 10 weeks were instrumental in proving to myself that I could do the job and be successful at it.

Recommendation 3: Resilience, Determination, and Grit

If you are accepted into the corps, an administrator will likely criticize you harshly at some point. There will be times when you have to work until 3:00 a.m. to get something done for your next day of class. You have to be able to respond positively and not take offense to the criticism, and put in the effort to finish your lesson plan when needed. You will need to constantly work to improve your teaching style. To some degree, the ability to fight through these obstacles has to be an inherent part of who you are. That doesn't mean that you have to be a strong Type A personality. There are, in fact, many different personality traits that lend themselves to a successful corps member who perseveres through challenges. It does mean, though, that you will have to overcome your fear of confrontation, failure, and voicing your opinion publicly. Whether you are charismatic is irrelevant; you simply have to know how to fight for what is right.

It's all about perseverance and resilience in Teach For America. While the organization might not concede directly that these are the most essential qualities of a strong leader, any teacher will tell you how important it is to have the resilience, determination, and grit to fight through every challenge you face. (Your interviewers will most likely be former corps members, so they know all too well how important this is.)

> *"Be resilient. We exist as an organization because there is an unorganized, tumultuous, frustrating, and unacceptable status quo. The only way we can make any impact in the wake of these challenges is to be patient, resilient, and relentless for our kids."*
>
> —Marielena '09
>
> *"Dedication is essential. Teaching is a difficult profession that will require you to work long hours inside and outside of school."*
>
> —Alex '09

A 2011 article on education in *The New York Times*[2] looked into the research on the role of "grit" in education, conducted by Angela Duckworth, now an assistant professor of psychology at the University of Pennsylvania. As a Ph.D. student, Duckworth determined the quality of grit—defined as a combination of deep passion for an issue and dedication to achieving a mission within that issue, no matter what obstacles present themselves—to be the best predictor of student achievement. To measure this quality, she developed a test, the so-called "grit scale," which was then implemented in KIPP and other high-performing schools to determine which character traits to foster in students. Since then, David Levin, the cofounder of KIPP, has implemented character

---

2 Tough, Paul. 2011. "What if the Secret to Success is Failure?" *The New York Times*, www.nytimes.com.

building into his schools. He uses the terms "optimism," "curiosity," and "social intelligence" to complement grit, and has shown how the ability to persevere is often a better indication of success than IQ.[3]

Dominic Randolph, also featured in the article, is the headmaster at New York's prestigious Riverdale Country School. He asked Duckworth to administer the grit scale for his students. A self-proclaimed skeptic about traditional American education, Randolph lends a lot of insight to current education theory, albeit from a very different perspective:

> Whether it's the pioneer in the Conestoga wagon or someone coming here in the 1920s from southern Italy, there was this idea in America that if you worked hard and you showed real grit, that you could be successful. Strangely, we've now forgotten that. People who have an easy time of things, who get 800s on their SAT's, I worry that those people get feedback that everything they're doing is great. And I think as a result, we are actually setting them up for long-term failure. When that person suddenly has to face up to a difficult moment, then I think they're screwed, to be honest. I don't think they've grown the capacities to be able to handle that.[4]

To connect this back to Recommendation 1, Randolph concludes in the article that in order to build grit, students must learn how to fail.

How You Can Develop This Skill/Experience

In the previous chapter, we talked about how to present perseverance and resilience in your application and interviews, but how do you build the skills themselves? Look back at the goals we laid out in the previous two sections, especially in the section on failure. I mean it when I say to go out and try one or more of those activities. They are not exercises in futility; they will help you learn to be resilient and persevere because you will have to use these traits to succeed. Don't give yourself excuses, because those won't be an option when it comes time for you to complete difficult tasks that have a real impact on children.

---

3 Tough, Paul. 2011. "What if the Secret to Success is Failure?" *The New York Times*, www.nytimes.com.

4 Ibid.

If you are working on becoming a good enough artist to sell your work, don't let an 8:00 a.m. class stop you. If you are training to run a marathon, don't let yourself deviate from your schedule for even one day, even if friends are visiting or you have a cold. If you are learning music theory, don't belittle your music classes at the expense of the classes in your major; treat them as equally important and excel in all of them.

The best way to stay on path and not give up is to plan the entire process in a detailed and meaningful way. This is also a great way to learn how to plan backward, as discussed in Chapter 3. So, if your goal is to become a good enough artist to sell your work, here are the questions you should ask yourself in each stage of the planning process.

Step 1: What do I want to accomplish at the end of the project? What does it mean to accomplish that goal?

- How do I determine what will be a successful sale of a piece of my art?

Step 2: How will I know that I have accomplished that goal? What does success actually look like?

- What does it mean to me to actually sell a piece of my art?
- How will I know when a piece of my art has sold?

Step 3: How will I get to that goal? What are the steps, in order, that need to happen to succeed?

- What is the most appropriate class in which I should enroll right now?
- How much time will I have to put in from now until I can sell the art?
- How will I sell my art? Through word of mouth? On a sidewalk? Through a coffee-shop gallery? By setting up a makeshift studio? Online?

Step 4: What kinds of actions do I need to take to accomplish each of those steps?

These questions expand on each of the questions from Step 3:

What is the most appropriate class in which I should enroll right now? From what level am I starting? Which style of art should I pursue? Does my college offer that class, or do I need to look for courses outside my school? Who can I talk to for an honest appraisal of my talent now? Is there a course catalogue that outlines a traditional path through a subject?

How much time will I have to put in from now until I can sell the art? How many classes do I anticipate needing? How much time do I have left in college to pursue these classes? How often should I work on my art each week? Who can help me estimate how much time I will need?

How will I sell my art? Where do young artists tend to sell their work? How do they market themselves? Where does my style of art most fit in? Do I know any artists who could help me get my work into a gallery or studio?

When you plan out your pursuit, you should actually answer your questions, not just ask them. You should also plot them out on a calendar or in some other structured way that works for you, so you can understand the entire process. Once laid out, the most important thing is to stick to the plan no matter what. You have decided that you are going to accomplish this task, so do it. Do not give up.

Recommendation 4: Understanding How Race, Class, and Privilege Affect Opportunity and the Current Education Landscape

This concept is very different from understanding and working with children. This is more focused on the macro level: understanding what is currently happening in education in this country and how that is interrelated with poverty. When I wrote my letter of intent for my application, I remember describing education as the civil rights issue of our generation, and wanting to join Teach For America to be at the front and center of that battle. Well, after two years in the classroom and another year of working with students through various nonprofits, I have been shocked by just how critical the situation really is. Education inequity is in unprecedented territory, and it is truly the civil rights issue of the new millennium.

> *"Take classes that talk about race and class frankly, honestly, and without academic pretension."*
>
> —Shane '09
>
> *"Read about the history of the city you will be going to. For example, read* A Prayer for the City *by H.G. Bissinger if you are coming to Philadelphia. There are many other great books that will give a cultural context of Philadelphia, and I am certain you will find the same for other regions."*
>
> —Alyson '02
>
> *"Become informed—learn as much about the state of education inequity in this nation and your city as you can."*
>
> —Mel '09
>
> *"Interested applicants should take a sociology/identity course on inequalities. Many corps members come in without the cultural competencies necessary to adjust to an environment where they will likely be the minority."*
>
> —Sarah '09

Understanding How Race, Class, and Privilege Affect Opportunity

Race, class, and socioeconomic status are difficult topics. They are all undoubtedly a major source of the tremendous wage gap and achievement gap that we see today, and although we are progressing as a society in these areas, we are still far from the finish line. This is one of the reasons that education reform is such a difficult topic. While there are many, many families who are able to overcome tremendous obstacles caused by poverty and racism to ensure that their children receive the opportunities they deserve, far too many hard-working families are not able to overcome these challenges. The fact is that prejudice and racism are still problems in the United States today, creating cycles of poverty from which it is hard to break free. Understanding some of the socioeconomic reasons why your students face the obstacles that they do is essential.

The majority of Teach For America corps members do not come from the type of environment in which they teach, although this is a smaller majority than in previous years. Teach For America is working hard to become more diverse. The organization recognizes the importance of having a wide range of backgrounds, experiences, races, and socioeconomic levels, and over the past few years has made expanding its diversity a priority. In the 2012 corps, 38 percent of incoming teachers identify as people of color, 35 percent come from low-income backgrounds, and 23 percent are the first in their families to earn a college degree.

However, it is a bit of a culture shock to some when they walk into the classroom for the first time. Having experience working with children is undoubtedly the best way to limit the difficulty of that transition, but it is also important to understand why our society is where it is today and how to overcome any unintended prejudices you may have.

How You Can Develop This Skill/Experience

If you are concerned about your ability to grasp how much race and class structures have impacted poverty, make a list of your university's departments that discuss race, poverty, and education (sociology, African-American studies, cultural studies, education, etc.). Ask friends majoring in those fields to recommend great professors and sign up for one of their classes. Try to find a class that has at most 30 students so that it will be more of a discussion or seminar than a lecture.

When you are in the class, do not treat it as just another elective you have to take to fulfill a requirement. Use this opportunity to speak at length with your professors and other students in the class about overcoming stereotypes, biases, and prejudices. Go to the professor's office hours and tell him you want to speak openly and candidly about these issues. Poverty, race, and prejudice are sensitive issues, and you may feel awkward initiating the conversation, but a good professor will welcome the opportunity to have a dialogue with an interested and engaged student. Most likely, the professor will be able to put your nerves at ease and provide you with the meaningful conversation you are seeking.

Having unintended prejudices or subconscious biases is perhaps inevitable for everyone, even if you mean well and regardless of your background. The key is to recognize it and have honest conversations about understanding and overcoming it. The more you can understand what poverty looks like, why it has evolved to where it is, and how you can work to understand that development, the more in tune with your students you will be.

Current Education Landscape

Ninety-four percent of Teach For America corps members did not major in education as undergraduates.[5] For an organization that works to improve education in our country, that number is pretty staggering. Many applicants have gained an understanding for these topics by studying anthropology, political science, or other social sciences, but they may not have examined education specifically. While I agree with Teach For America that a person's major does not affect her ability to be effective in the classroom, I find the lack of understanding that many incoming teachers have about the complexities of the current education landscape to be problematic. Many corps members have spent their college days becoming extracurricular leaders, taking finance classes, studying anthropology in Africa, struggling with organic chemistry, and learning communication and writing skills. They have the skills to be great teachers but little knowledge of the field. As anyone in business will tell you, you cannot fully know the market if you don't understand the industry.

We are at a critical point in the history of education in the United States. More students are in school than ever before. At the same time, billions of dollars are being cut from education across the nation. A high school degree is essentially a requirement for the most mundane unskilled jobs, and a college degree is now expected for almost anything even slightly above that.

---

5 "Who We Are," *Teach For* America, www.teachforamerica.org.

Low-income school districts, especially in urban centers, are getting hit the worst. For example, because of a looming $1.2 billion deficit projected by 2017, the School District of Philadelphia is all but disbanding. In 2013, the school district will close 40 public schools, and then close 32 more by 2017. Unbelievably, this might actually be the only logical action the district can take. Many of its schools have been failing for years, making drastic measures inevitable. There is an inherent problem in the system when closing 72 schools and displacing tens of thousands of students becomes the best option.

How You Can Develop This Skill/Experience

Try to come into the corps with a good understanding of the status quo in education and what people are doing to overcome it. The problem with education, though, is that it is not a black-and-white issue. There is no "for" and "against" as in other controversial topics like abortion or same-sex marriage. Education is a supremely complicated issue, and it is difficult to figure out where to begin.

To understand the current landscape, do some research on popular education issues like pre-K education, school choice and vouchers, public vs. charter schools, teachers' unions, seniority-based layoffs, teacher evaluation, merit-based pay, standardized testing, school autonomy, tenure, and data-driven instruction. On every one of these issues (and countless others), there are people vehemently fighting on both sides, yet there isn't necessarily a "right" or "wrong" answer to any of them. As you learn more and more, you should start to develop your own vision of what you think is the best path to improving the education sector. Most likely, the answer involves a combination of these topics and many more.

It is also likely that there are some very relevant and interesting policies and actions being discussed locally in your city or state. While you do not yet know where you will be placed if accepted, you do know where you will be interviewing. Do some research on local education issues and policies affecting that region. This research will also help illustrate your dedication to the movement, especially if you can speak intelligently during the interview about current education policy, both nationally and locally. If you live in Chicago, for example, your interviewer likely works on the staff of the Teach For America–Chicago office. She knows the trends and will be impressed if you have taken the initiative to learn about them.

The bottom line is, the more you can start wrapping your brain around the complex issue that is the current education landscape, the better prepared you will be to set foot in the classroom for the first time and understand why things are happening the way they are. You will likely see inefficiency and seemingly illogical decisions often in your school, and it will be quite confusing if you don't understand why they are happening. Everything you will see stems from previous decisions made and actions taken long before you got there.

I would recommend picking up a couple books, finding a good online blog, or at least keeping up with the local newspaper to get a sense of the education landscape locally. When you are placed in a region, you will be immediately immersed in the education politics there, and having an informed opinion coming in will help you understand them even better.

In Appendix 1 you will find a list of books that discuss all of these various issues. I am neither supporting nor refuting the arguments made in any of them. In fact, it is important to hear arguments from both sides to truly develop your understanding of the issue. If possible, I recommend reading at least two or three of these books, preferably on different topics or exhibiting different opinions, before your interviews. There are also a number of books on the list that will help you understand the issues of poverty and racism in the United States discussed earlier in the chapter.

Recommendation 5: Flexibility and the Locus of Control

Flexibility means being open-minded enough with your placement, school, classroom, and students to understand that not everything will work perfectly every time. You must realize that you have chosen to join a system that is often stretched to the limit. You must have an open mind, both at the classroom level and at the school operations level, or you will not be as effective a teacher as you could be.

If you are accepted into the program, you will quickly learn about the "locus of control," one of the many key phrases within Teach For

America's terminology. Locus of control was the concept that stuck with me and many other corps members the most. This phrase essentially means that you have the ability to directly control some things, but there is a lot over which you have no control, and you should not spend time or energy on things that you cannot influence. Corps members should spend all of their time perfecting the "controllable" space and not letting unavoidable problems get in the way. Trying to solve unsolvable problems will not only make you frustrated, but will cost you valuable time as well.

"Incoming corps members need to be adaptive to change. Teaching in a failing school district requires that you have a plan A, a plan B, a plan C, and a plan D, but most of the time you have to throw them all out and start from scratch. If you can't handle that, teaching will be very difficult for you."

—Joanna '09

"I had no idea what my placement would be or what teaching would be like, but I fully expected it to be incredibly difficult, and I am certain that expectation helped me through the first year. When the work felt nearly impossible, I acknowledged the situation and did the best I could. With that attitude, I was able to be flexible when new, unexpected situations came up. You really have to roll with the various obstacles that are thrown at you and adjust your plan. You can't predict or plan for everything, but you can control how you react and think about each situation. Be ready to adjust your mindset and expectations, because it will be hard to predict exactly what will happen."

—Kate '10

> *"I think that incoming corps members must enter this semi-broken system realizing that there are a thousand pieces to the puzzle, some of which are missing. Incoming corps members should not take on the weight of a crumbling district, but should navigate through the chaos knowing their 'locus of control,' supports, and what they themselves are capable of accomplishing inside the classroom on a daily basis. Yes, they are responsible for their students' achievement. No, they are not responsible for the climate and politics in the city's schools."*
>
> —Lauren '09

Flexibility

You must be flexible with what is given to you (or thrown at you), recognize what you can and cannot control, and keep on the best course for the kids. You might go through three or four different rosters during the first couple months of school (I had three in my first year). You might not even have a school placement until you are a week into the school year. Teach For America might tell you that you will be teaching seventh-grade science, but your school needs you to teach eighth-grade math. Schools and classrooms, no matter what they look like and no matter how well the kids buy in, will never run 100 percent smoothly all of the time. While it is essential to be consistent in your classroom management so that your students have clear expectations, being too inflexible can derail a class or alienate a student. Roll with the punches and keep focused on your students' success.

How You Can Develop This Skill/Experience

Living with people of different backgrounds, studying abroad in a non-Western country, and rebounding from failures with a positive attitude and new ideas are great ways to develop flexibility. If you built this ability through a tangible action or experience, you can talk about it in your interviews. You can also develop flexibility on an ongoing basis through your personal life. Compromise with family, friends, and roommates more often and work on seeing things from their perspective.

In terms of what you can do right now, let's return to the activity you chose to pursue earlier in this chapter and the plan you created. As the weeks go on and you work through the plan, reflect on your progress and re-evaluate your direction. For example, you will have to change paths if you were arranging to sell your art through a friend's gallery, but she decided to close it down. Instead of giving up and blaming her, you just need to find a new place to promote your work. Perhaps, after one photography class you realize that you do not get along with the teacher, but you have really enjoyed a few conversations with a painting professor. You may want to re-evaluate your decision to pursue photography and instead take an Introduction to Painting class, even if it sets your plan back a couple of months. If you are much more likely to be successful with this new teacher, then that may be a better path. While perseverance is essential, you cannot be so headstrong that you continue down a failing path. Being flexible means altering your path when you know you are pursuing the wrong one.

Locus of Control

Teach For America applicants are used to being in control of and excelling in everything they do. In college, in many work situations, and even in one's personal life, there is little that cannot be controlled to at least some degree. But in the classroom, it is important to be aware of what you can directly control and what you cannot control. Misusing your time can have drastic consequences on your students' outcomes, and some of the most time-consuming and frustrating situations occur when attempting to solve an unsolvable problem. When faced with one of these situations, you must learn how to work alongside or within the obstacle so that you spend your energy working on challenges that you can control.

How You Can Develop This Skill/Experience

You can become more aware of the locus of control in your life by using what I call a "happiness/unhappiness" chart. First, draw a line down the center of a piece of paper. On the left side, write "happy" and on the right side, write "unhappy." Now, list everything in your life right now that makes you excited, joyful, or grateful on the left side and everything that makes you anxious, sad, or angry on the right side. Keep in mind that these can be personal, professional, or academic and should include things that you can and cannot control. Be brutally honest with yourself; if your lifelong best friend actually brings you down and makes you feel unhappy, even if you have never admitted it to anyone, put her on the "unhappy" list.

Once you have done that, go through both lists. Cross out everything over which you have no control. Again, be honest. If you do have control over something but feel it would be very hard to change, you should not draw a line through it.

Take a look at what you did not cross out on your "happy" list. Those are the people, things, activities, and places that you have decided to consciously pursue because they bring you joy. You should actively work on improving your relationship with those parts of your life. Now look at what you did not cross off the "unhappy" list. Those are the people, things, activities, and places that you have decided to pursue, but that bring down your quality of life. If you did this exercise correctly, you have the ability to either change your interaction with them or cut them out of your life entirely.

Finally, take a look at what you crossed out on both lists. Those are the parts of your life over which you truly have no control, and about which there is no use worrying. For the crossed-out items on the "happy" list, appreciate them to the fullest but don't worry about them going away. You have no control anyway, so enjoy them for what they are. For the crossed-out items on the "unhappy" list, there is absolutely no reason to spend any time or mental anguish thinking about them. They will be there regardless, so it is best to manage them in the best way you can and focus on improving what you can control.

When you are a teacher, you can do a similar exercise with "positives" and "negatives" in your classroom.

Final Thought

We have talked a lot about what it means to have the potential to be a strong leader in Teach For America. I have given you many examples of the different qualities, skills, and experiences the organization looks for in its candidates, and have shown you how to both build them in your own life and exhibit them most effectively when communicating your accomplishments.

The second part of the book will show you how to take these leadership roles and accomplishments that you have achieved and use them to craft the most compelling application possible. As you fill out your application and interact with interviewers in the phone and final interviews, keep in mind the seven core competencies and additional skills and experiences discussed in Part 1 of this book. If you are able to represent yourself as someone with high potential to be a leader by exhibiting all of these qualities, then you have an excellent chance of being admitted to the corps.

Understanding the Teaching Profession

One of the key things an individual can do to prepare for teaching is to truly understand what a craft teaching is. My biggest advice is to observe an instructor who has been classified as excellent in a public school, charter school, parochial school, independent school, and alternative high school, and also to review a few teacher performance evaluation standards. One example is the Danielson Model, which outlines the skills of a true educator. Reading about this will allow you to appreciate just how hard this profession is to master, and to understand that there is always room for improvement.

A classroom is never just four walls; there is also a door through which your students will walk each day. When they leave your class, they will walk into the community in which many of them have grown up. That community has a history. As a teacher, you need to understand the background, families, and stories that built that community. When you enter your school, talk to the veteran teachers about the school's history and reputation and ask families about the community because it is essential to know what your kids are bringing through that door. While you will never be able to walk every step with them, you can work to understand the context and learn from it. When you teach, pull from this understanding. Constantly strive to learn from the halls, streets, and porches that surround your school.

Too often, young people come into this field with lower expectations of what it takes to be a great teacher. The reality is that teaching is one of the hardest professions out there, and the "GREATS"—the ones who inspired us to go into education ourselves—have put in endless time, study, and practice to improve their craft. You must do the same. There will always be a new student to challenge your approach and your skills, and you will have to adapt to meet these new challenges. Understanding and respecting how truly challenging this profession is will push you to meet the learning needs of your students.

—Alyson Goodner (Bay Area '02)

PART 2:

Recruiting,

Applying, and

Interviewing

Chapter 5

The Recruitment Process

Unlike many other competitive jobs or schools you may be considering, getting a recommendation from a recruiter or knowing someone in Teach For America will not directly help your chances of getting accepted into the corps. Because the selection process is 100 percent research-based and standardized, connections do not play a role in the process. The selection team will never know whether you were recruited or not, so your application will not be at a direct disadvantage if your school does not have a recruitment team or if you are unable to secure a meeting.

Furthermore, the recruitment team is not able to give you personalized feedback on your application or candidacy. The reason to meet with a recruiter is to learn more about the organization, familiarize yourself with the way Teach For America operates and communicates, and ask any questions that you may have. While this may seem trivial and unimportant, internalizing the nuances of the organization and interacting with people who have spent years in the classroom and on staff can give you enormous insight for your application and interviews.

This chapter will focus on helping you understand what the recruitment team looks like, how Teach For America evaluates prospects, how to secure a meeting with the recruitment manager, and what kinds of questions you should ask her during the meeting to gain as much insight and knowledge as possible.

Recruitment Team

The recruitment team has several goals, but at its core, the team strives to find strong and diverse leaders on campus and encourage them to apply. There are three main positions on any given campus recruitment team: recruitment manager (RM), recruitment associate (RA), and campus campaign coordinator (CCC). The team's presence on campus will depend on the prominence and size of your school; high-target colleges (e.g., Ivy League schools, Duke, Northwestern, Wellesley) and top state universities (e.g., Michigan, UC Berkeley, Virginia) will have large teams, while lesser-known schools may not have a recruitment team at all.

To give you some perspective on size, I was a CCC when I was a senior at the University of California, Santa Barbara (UCSB), the year before I began my commitment as a corps member. UCSB is by no means an Ivy League school, but it is a part of the University of California system. Our team had one RM, one RA, and between two and five CCCs, depending on the time of year (our team dwindled as the recruitment season came to a close). We were also in charge of recruiting from a number of nearby universities, including Cal State Bakersfield and UC Merced. I was one of the last two CCCs who finished out the year, so I was part of the team from start to finish.[1]

Recruitment Manager (RM)

The RM leads the recruitment campaign on campus. She is ultimately responsible for ensuring that recruitment benchmarks are met by various deadlines and that the recruitment campaign runs smoothly. All other team members report directly to her. Her biggest job is meeting individually with dozens of highly qualified potential applicants per day in 15- to 30-minute sessions. She also runs information sessions on campus. When needed, she may fill in to do classroom presentations or pass out flyers (usually handled by CCCs). The RM is an alumnus of the program, although she may not have been on the Teach For America staff for long.

Recruitment Associate (RA)

The RA performs most of the behind-the-scenes work. Because much of this work is electronic, the RA may not even live in the city in which the team is based. The RA will email potential applicants to set up meetings and answer any general questions. He will send out information to

---

1 To give my teammates a little shout-out: Our recruitment team at UCSB ranked second nationwide in percentage growth of accepted applicants from 2008 to 2009.

students who have signed up at career fairs, class presentations, or tables on campus. He may also email students who have been identified as potentially strong applicants, but who have not yet shown interest in applying to Teach For America. The RA is in direct communication with the CCCs on logistical matters and can be a resource for them when the RM is not available. The RA may or may not have been a corps member. As a candidate, you will probably interact a great deal with the RA by email, but will likely never meet him in person.

Campus Campaign Coordinator (CCC)

The CCCs do most of the groundwork for the campaign. They are juniors or seniors enrolled at the university where they work. To get the job, they have both shown early interest in Teach For America and proven that they can identify and access networks of students at their school deemed to be high-potential applicants. The CCCs spend much of their time identifying potential applicants and ranking students who have shown interest. They dig through department websites to find the top students in each major, glean more information about the leadership backgrounds of students on honors lists and in honors societies, and reach out to professors and other students for recommendations. They also schedule talks and present about Teach For America in classrooms likely to have highly qualified candidates. They input potential applicants into a database, which the RM and RA then use to schedule meetings. CCCs are still undergraduate students, so they have not served as corps members, although many CCCs do end up applying.

Targeting Potential Applicants

Recruitment works as a sort of pre-selection process. While the recruitment department and the selection department of Teach For America are separate, and the metrics each of them uses to evaluate potential applicants are not exactly the same, there is an obvious correlation between the two. The more impressive your resume and background, the more likely you are to meet with a recruitment manager and the more likely you are to be accepted.

Members of the recruitment team look anywhere and everywhere to find students who have impressive resumes. During my time as a CCC, I performed detailed searches on thousands of students. While this may sound a bit invasive, it is no different than what recruiters for any competitive organization do when looking for potential recruits. With the amount of information now in the public domain, we wanted to know that someone at least had the potential to get accepted before we spent 15–30 minutes meeting with him. Many times, I searched friends who initially seemed like strong applicants, only to learn through research that they really had no chance of acceptance, so they were never contacted about a meeting.

When I got the name of someone from a sign-in sheet, honors list, or some other source, I would search for him on Facebook and LinkedIn and cross-check the information with a Google search and a scan of the person's academic department website. I would then search for associations with extracurricular activities like the Greek system, religious organizations, student government, and other on-campus groups. This process would take anywhere from thirty seconds to four minutes, depending on how available the information was. I rarely spent more than three or four minutes on one person.[2] I would then enter all of the information I found into a database, and the RA and RM would use that information to reach out to students and set up meetings.

Here are examples of students who had a high likelihood, a medium likelihood, and a low likelihood of getting accepted into Teach For America. After reviewing the qualifications of each student, assign yourself to one of the three groups. Be honest with yourself when figuring out where you fall; your recruiters and interviewers will be objective, so it only hurts you to be biased. This list alone might tell you whether it is worth putting in the effort to apply to the corps.

---

2 Keep in mind that this was what we did in 2008–2009, and the Internet has become even more important since then.

High Likelihood

- *Sean*
  - 3.76 GPA
  - Pre-med major
  - President of the student body (senior year)
  - Organized and led a group of 22 pre-med majors to Panama for a week-long medical workshop in a rural village during spring break of his junior year

- *Julie*
  - 3.41 GPA
  - Political science and finance double major
  - Worked 40 hours per week throughout college to pay for school
  - Founded the Black Student Congress as a freshman, which she expanded to 14 nearby colleges over a three-year period. The Black Student Congress now has a total of 5,600 members.

- *Vanessa*
  - 3.96 GPA
  - Business major with a concentration in finance
  - President of Chi Omega sorority
  - Member of Phi Beta Kappa honors society

- *Robert*
  - 3.79 GPA
  - Communications major
  - Captain of the baseball team, conference champions for the last two years

Medium Likelihood

- *Carl*
  - 3.21 GPA
  - Engineering and education double major

- Manages a team of 10 volunteers through a local organization that goes into middle schools two days per week and teaches engineering to eighth graders
- Head server at a popular local restaurant, working 20 hours per week to help pay for college and managing 7 other servers

- *Jessica*
  - 3.60 GPA
  - Sociology major
  - Treasurer of Real Life, a Christian organization on campus with 350 members

- *Johnny*
  - 3.52 GPA
  - Vice president of Alpha Tau Omega fraternity
  - Business economics major

Low Likelihood

- *Christina*
  - 3.13 GPA
  - Pre-law major
  - Big Brothers Big Sisters mentor
  - Columnist for the school newspaper

- *Mike*
  - 3.43 GPA
  - Math major with a minor in electrical engineering (very little involvement outside of his coursework)

- *Rachel*
  - 2.76 GPA
  - Communications major
  - Member of Hillel

Now, this is just a baseline level for these potential candidates. Regardless of where you fall, you will have to take the application and interviews very seriously. There are many applicants in the "high likelihood" category who are not accepted and applicants in the "low likelihood" category who are accepted, just as there are students with perfect 2400 SAT scores who are rejected from Harvard and students with SAT scores far below the median who are accepted. Don't think that you are a shoo-in just because you are in the "high likelihood" category, or that you have no chance at acceptance because you are in the "low likelihood" category.

How to Increase Your Visibility

The biggest question, now, is how to place yourself so that the recruitment team identifies you as someone with whom the recruitment manager wants to meet. There are two ways to present yourself so that they actively seek you out. The first, and best, way is to interact directly with the Teach For America recruitment team as much as possible. The second is to develop your online presence so that your accomplishments are easy to find when searching online.

Interact with Teach For America

Interacting with Teach For America as much as possible is the best way to get on the recruitment team's radar and learn about the organization. The recruitment team spends a lot of time and energy marketing the organization on campus and hosting information sessions for interested applicants. They pass out flyers, occupy booths at career fairs, and hold presentations in classrooms with sign-in sheets. You should take advantage of all opportunities to interact with them. Sign in *every time* you come into contact with a sign-in sheet and include any information they request, such as GPA or associations. The more times you sign in, the more they will note your interest, which may signal to the RA to contact you.

The absolute best way to get on Teach For America's radar is to attend information sessions. The recruitment manager will lead the session, talk about her experiences as a teacher, and give general advice on applying. After the session, she will answer questions from the group about logistics, the application, and the interviews. This is a great way to get your general questions answered and hear answers to questions you may not have thought of on your own.

However, the Q&A is not the place to have more personal questions answered, or to spend time interacting directly with the recruiters. You should go to the information session 15 minutes early, prepared with specific questions for the RM. The recruitment team will likely start preparing for the event at least an hour early, and the last 15 minutes before the event are usually spent waiting around and finishing any last-minute details.

If the information session includes an alumni panel, you have even more incentive to get there early. For alumni panels, the recruitment team brings together a number of current or former corps members from your school or region. This is a great opportunity to meet people who come from your college or city and have succeeded in the application process. If you can find out ahead of time who the alumni are and what they are doing, you can prepare specific questions to ask each of them. If one of the speakers is on Teach For America's staff, it is possible that she will be a part of the selection team as well. Imagine the peace of mind you would have if you walk into the final interview not only having had an extensive conversation with one of the interviewers, but also having shown her your interest in the organization and dedication to the movement.

Create an Online Presence

It is important for recruiters to be able to easily find out about every impressive thing you have done. Remember, when searching online, recruiters rarely spend more than three or four minutes on any one person. If they cannot find everything in that time, they will assume it does not exist and move on. What is available to the public, positive and negative, is immensely important in today's world. Forget about the whole privacy thing; our world is no longer private. Having your information out there for the world to see can and should be a *good* thing.

You need to create an online presence for yourself so that when a recruiter searches for you, he is quickly impressed and wants to pursue a meeting. If the recruiter can't find anything more than basic information about you, he may just enter you as a low-target prospect and move on. For example, if all he knows is that you are in a sorority, he will base his entire entry on that. You may have been instrumental in founding an on-campus organization and have a 3.9 GPA, but he does not know that if it is not easily accessible.

To revamp your online presence, you will need to do some in-depth googling of your name and know exactly what your public and friend (or equivalent) profiles look like on Facebook, LinkedIn, Twitter, Tumblr, YouTube, Foursquare, Yelp, Instagram, Flickr, and anything else you can imagine. I am going to walk you through the process of developing your online presence in detail for Facebook and LinkedIn, as they are the most important, and briefly for the rest of the sites. You do not want a bland, cookie-cutter online persona; you want to make it as impressive as possible. That doesn't mean putting on a suit for every single picture you put online. It means allowing people to get a positive impression of you, not a neutral or negative one.

Google

The very first thing you need to do is determine what information about you is out there. First, log out of all social networking sites and campus logins. You want to see what an average person will see, not what you see. Next, do a simple Google search for your name and all relevant groups with which you associate. The goal is to see what shows up in the search results and then work to make those sites as strong as possible.

In my own case, I might search with this combination of keywords to get an overview of my online presence (hint: use a "+" in between your name and keywords):

- "Jake Whitman"
- "Jake Whitman + Teach For America"
- "Jake Whitman + Philadelphia" *(my current city)*
- "Jake Whitman + Cincinnati" *(my hometown)*

- "Jake Whitman + UCSB" *(my alma mater)*
- "Jake Whitman + Santa Barbara"
- "Jake Whitman + Business Economics" *(my major in college)*
- "Jake Whitman + awards"
- "Jake Whitman + education"
- "Jake Whitman + book"
- "Jake Whitman + Facebook"

Scroll through a few pages for each search. Open pages like Facebook, LinkedIn, and other results that mention your name. Look at the images under Google's "Images" tab. You want to get a comprehensive picture of what people find when they only have basic information about you.

Next, enter everything you find on yourself in an Excel spreadsheet. In one column, copy and paste the URL for each site that mentions your name. To the right of each URL, enter what the site says about you. Time for more brutal honesty: Using only this information, decide whether you have a high, medium, or low likelihood of being accepted. Again, don't be biased; the recruiters won't know any more about you at this point. This is your benchmark.

Once you have completed this task, you want to split up the lists into sites over which you have direct control (e.g., Facebook, LinkedIn, Twitter) and those over which you do not (e.g., university department page, employment pages). Now, let's look at each of the sites you can control.

Facebook

Think of Facebook as both a social vehicle to communicate with friends and a way to market yourself online. Your friends may not look at your "About Me" section very often, but recruiters certainly will. You want your Facebook profile to be impressive and straightforward, with your experiences, accomplishments, and associations explicitly and clearly stated.

This is how to view your Facebook profile as someone other than yourself:

- Go to your Timeline

- Find a little asterisk with an arrow next to the "Activity Log" button. Click that and then click "View as..."

- To see how the public views your profile (non-friends), click the blue "public" link at the top. To see how friends see your profile, just type in the name of a friend who is not on any kind of limited profile and hit "Enter."

This is important: When updating your public profile, *make sure that you are searchable*. It is pointless to create a strong profile if a recruiter cannot find you. Go to your privacy settings and make sure that your profile is searchable and visible to everyone.

For both your public and friend profiles, analyze your Facebook presence. You should ask these questions:

- What does the "About" section say about me?

- What else can I add from my experiences or involvements that will make my profile more impressive?

- What sorts of organizations or clubs am I associated with? What groups do I like? If I am directly affiliated with those groups, am I listed on their pages?

- What have I posted on my wall lately?

- What have my friends posted on my wall lately?

- What kinds of pictures show up? Are all of my pictures, only my previous profile pictures, or none of my pictures visible?

You likely need to revamp your Facebook profile for both types of viewers. My recommendation is to make it the same for everyone; you shouldn't have anything on your Facebook page that could jeopardize your reputation, and you never know if one of your "friends" will be searching for you. But the degree to which you open your profile to the public or close it to your friends is ultimately up to you. If you would rather let your friends, but not the public, see your pictures, change your settings to reflect that. You must, though, have a public profile that people can easily find, so that someone who does not know you can find you and quickly see a snapshot of what you have accomplished. Facebook alone may get you a meeting with the RM.

To enhance your "About" section, take out your resume and start entering your information. Think back to Chapter 3, when we discussed using measurable and quantitative examples to illustrate your experiences. Employers should be listed in reverse chronological order, with your title and a blurb that details exactly what you do or did with that organization. Use titles that reveal your leadership responsibilities and enter information that will impress a recruiter. Don't lie, but make sure you don't diminish your responsibilities and accomplishments either. This is not the time to be humble.

Make sure that your college information is up to date. Include your degree (B.A., B.S., etc.), your major(s), and any minor(s). In the description field, include your current cumulative GPA and major GPA if it is higher. Enter any honors programs, awards, or dean's list mentions you have earned. If you studied abroad, include the school where you studied. If you held any leadership positions or had any unique experiences while abroad, be sure to enter those in the description as well. Anything helps that paints a better picture of who you are.

Your "About" section is most important, but don't underestimate your pictures. You don't need pictures of modeling or speaking at an event, but try to avoid using your profile pictures to memorialize that night you drank too much tequila. In fact, if you have any of those pictures up, delete or hide them immediately. At your age, and as an aspiring teacher, Facebook is no longer the place to showcase those photos.

LinkedIn

While Facebook is the most ubiquitous social media platform, LinkedIn is the most important to use to your advantage. It is also probably the most underutilized. Why? Because it's not fun like Facebook or Twitter. Posting pictures of your friends is amusing. Writing out your resume is tedious and difficult. Friending that cute guy you met last night is fun. Connecting through a website with your new coworker seems unimportant. However, LinkedIn is the best place for a recruiter to get detailed information about your accomplishments and experiences.

LinkedIn is an amazing resource. It is a place for you to put your resume, CV, cover letter, and interests all in one place. There is no stigma against using more than a certain number of pages or words (like there is with a resume or cover letter), and you are free to include whatever you want. You can show your connections with important people and ask them to write recommendations about you. You can reach out to corps members and Teach For America staff with whom you might want to talk. LinkedIn is the ultimate networking community and should be used as such.

It is very likely that you have information missing in your LinkedIn profile. Set aside a couple of hours one evening after class to update your profile. Luckily, LinkedIn has a great tracking tool that tells you what percentage of your profile is complete. Try to get the bar to 100 percent.

First, sign in to your LinkedIn profile or create an account. Then, follow the steps below.

Email Address Contacts

To find all of your connections on LinkedIn, enter all email addresses you use. LinkedIn will match the contact lists from your email against its database and find your contacts' profiles on its network. Invite everyone you know to connect with you and spend time looking at their connections to find additional people you know.

Industry

Enter the industry that best matches your major or your professional interests. Don't worry about making it "education" if you feel that your industry is something else.

Resume

Once you have finished all of the initial questions from LinkedIn, the biggest step is uploading your resume. This will fill in all information for job experience, education, and other fields. You may edit the fields to include more or less information as needed. As there are no structure or page limits, you can be more descriptive than you are in your resume.

Photo

Upload a professional headshot of yourself. Do not include friends in your picture and do not wear a T-shirt. If you don't have a headshot of yourself wearing business attire, get a friend to take one for you. Having a presentable photo is one of the best ways to gain people's trust.

Summary

The summary is essentially a mini cover letter. You want to give the reader a sense of who you are, what you have done, and what you are doing, especially if you have accomplishments or qualities that don't always show up in a traditional resume. Highlight leadership experiences and what they have meant to you. Include any striking quantitative data as well. Try to keep the summary to 150 words or fewer. Any more than that and you may lose the reader.

Experience

Your experience section should be virtually identical to your resume, with your work experience and leadership experience combined (you may want to read the section on resumes in Chapter 7 before continuing). Again, because you have no length limit, you can add a little more information if you think it would present a more comprehensive description of your position or accomplishments. Don't write a whole page describing each position, but if you need four bullet points, go for it.

Skills and Expertise

This section can seem a bit fluffy, but spend 10 minutes or so going through LinkedIn's list of skills and picking out the ones that apply most to you. While these may not be significant on their own, they are a nice way to present the things you know how to do well.

Education

Again, this section should look exactly like the education section at the top of your resume. You have room to enter your GPA, the activities and societies in which you participated, and any additional information, including all honors, awards, and other noteworthy accomplishments.

Recommendations

Recommendations are tricky, but they can be a great way to earn validation and legitimacy for the work you have accomplished. Try to get at least one recommendation from a colleague, friend, professor, or associate for each position you list, both professional and academic. Send someone a request through LinkedIn and then follow up with a personal email thanking him. You can also ask if he would rather have you draft a short recommendation that he can then edit and submit. This saves him time and will help you get a recommendation much more quickly.

Additional Information

Here you can add your personal or company website (or a website that highlights something you have accomplished), your Twitter handle, interests, groups and associations, and honors and awards. Enter anything you have done or are interested in that does not come up in other parts of your profile.

Personal Information

Only list personal information that you are comfortable displaying publicly. I do suggest that you list a phone number, although there are ways of getting around putting your real phone number online.[3] You should not list your real address. Whether you include your IM, birthday, and marital status is up to you. It won't help you or hurt you. If you would rather keep them private, leave them blank.

Once you enter all of this information, the gray "snapshot" box should populate. Check the information that is listed there and make any final changes where necessary.

---

3 Google Voice provides you with a free phone number that connects to your cell or landline phone but does not link to any personal information, thereby protecting your privacy.

Other Sites

You should do a similar type of analysis for all other websites and social platforms where you have direct control. Below are some short, general thoughts on a few of the other sites you may use.

Twitter

If you are an avid tweeter and it associates with your name in searches, make sure to keep your content relatively clean. You don't have to use Twitter as a marketing campaign for yourself, but you don't want it to damage your image either. Write a catchy and creative bio and make sure not to raise red flags with your posts.

Blogging Sites (Tumblr, Blogger, WordPress, etc.)

If you are a blogger, keep your content free of red flags, especially if you are using your real name. It does not look good when applying to Teach For America if your blog contains inappropriate material. Your blog is your space to really let people see who you are and what you are interested in, so stay away from disrespecting others, bragging about crimes committed, etc., even when joking. Those are things to be shared in private or not at all.

YouTube

If you have a YouTube account associated with your name, make sure the content is not harmful, or even the least bit unflattering. You would be surprised at how easy it is to find videos that people uploaded years ago, about which they have likely forgotten. Search your accounts and your friends' accounts for videos that are potentially harmful, and have them taken down or made private.

Yelp

If you are active on Yelp and like to write reviews that bash stores, restaurants, or businesses without real merit, you may want to rethink your methods. Teach For America doesn't want to hire someone who carelessly attacks others. If you want to write negative reviews, be respectful and informative.

Your Department's Website

Your department's website is obviously a place over which you do not have direct control, but it is a great platform to be highlighted on. When I was recruiting, I would go to every department's website and look at recent news about students. When I found names of students who had been awarded tremendous honors or done amazing things, I immediately put them in the database as strong potential applicants, even if this was the first time we had identified them. I know a number of students whom we contacted this way and who later applied and were accepted.

Here are two examples of online articles that mention students who achieved impressive things in their departments or in their school as a whole. I found these through a simple search of department websites of two different universities. To protect the identity of the students, I have slightly changed each article's title and removed all identifying information, including names and universities.

"Undergraduate Students Receive University Leadership Recognition"
—University Sociology Department, May 14, 2012

This article cites three students with concentrations in sociology who won prestigious awards. The first student won the "Senior of the Year" award and is the president of the Muslim Students Association. The second student was recognized as the "Most Impactful Student on Campus" for her work with two different student groups. The third student was selected to be a part of an elite Leadership Honor Society and will be the president of the Undergraduate Sociology Association. From this information, all three of these students seem to have a high likelihood of being accepted into Teach For America.

"Student Group Named among Nation's Best Innovators"
—College School of Engineering, February 22, 2012

This article highlights a number of students who run a hydropower organization that already operates internationally in developing countries. They presented their business plan at a national competition and were selected as semifinalists—one of 18 teams selected out of 200 participants. This is a remarkable accomplishment, as they were undoubtedly competing against some of the smartest people from around the country.

So, the question is, how do you do something that will get you highlighted on your department's website? There are two ways to go about it.

The easy way (although "easy" is a relative term) is to get involved in something impressive that is already happening. To find out about these opportunities, visit a department advisor and ask her what you can do to get more involved in leadership positions or groups in your major. Do a little research about what people are doing in your department and reference those when talking to the advisor. Advisors love students with passion and energy and will likely be eager to help you. If you would like to get involved with a specific project, ask the advisor to introduce you to the project founder or president.

The other option is to do something remarkable and then let your department know about it. Let's say in your attempt to learn how to fail, as discussed in Chapter 4, you start a nonprofit organization on microfinancing that really takes off. After months of preparation, you organize a group of college sophomores to go to Ghana for winter break to implement a sustainable micro-finance program. Go to your department and let them know about it! Before you go on the trip, ask if they would be willing to write a story about your program and what you do. While you are in Ghana, take a lot of pictures and notes. When you return, share these pictures and stories with your department and ask them to feature you in a follow-up article. If you are a finance major and I am the dean of the Business School, I would be jumping at the opportunity to highlight your nonprofit on the website.

Meeting with Recruitment Manager

Now that you have spent the time signaling to the recruitment manager that you are worth talking to, both through your direct interaction with the recruitment team and through your online presence, let's talk about the meeting itself. When the RA or RM emails you about setting up a meeting, check your calendar and promptly send him a few dates and times when you are available. If he is just reaching out to you to gauge your interest in the program, reply with a question or two about Teach For America and indicate that you would welcome the opportunity to meet with the RM to discuss the program in more detail. Be direct, honest, and clear with your objectives. The RA is emailing dozens of students every day, so the less back-and-forth, the better.

When you sit down to meet with the RM, come with an open mind and interested attitude. He will ask you about your past experiences and talk to you about the organization. He will help you understand why Teach For America is a great opportunity, and why he thinks you should apply. He will give you as much information as he can, although he is not supposed to give you direct personal feedback about your resume or your chance of acceptance.

In many ways, the RM is completely on your team. He wants to find strong candidates who ultimately get accepted, so he will be willing to serve as a resource whenever questions come up. RMs can introduce you to local corps members and alumni, answer general questions about the application and interview process, and answer questions about Teach For America as an organization and the kinds of experiences you should expect if you are accepted.

Whenever you speak with a recruiter, try to pick up on things he says that you can internalize and incorporate into your application and interviews. If he mentions a part of the mission that intrigues you, ask him to talk more about it and respond with any experiences you have that help you relate to that sentiment. If he gives you reasons he thinks your background or experiences would make you a strong candidate, tuck those away for future use. If he comments on your lack of leadership history, immediately think about exploring leadership options with an organization or company with which you are involved. Actively listening in this manner will help you understand what Teach For America values most, and it will serve you well to think along the same lines when you begin the application process.

The problem, though, is that recruitment managers have to stay fair among candidates and within their Teach For America boundaries, so to speak. This means that you may come away with answers to some of your questions, but they may not be quite as specific and satisfying as you would like. RMs aren't supposed to give you any feedback at all on your personal candidacy, so you very well could come out of the meeting learning nothing of substance. The key to getting advice that you can use is to ask the right questions. Here are a few questions that you can ask the RM that may help you gain information about your candidacy. These are not meant to somehow outsmart the RM; they are simply questions that you can ask for which the RM's response will likely include something of substance.

1. Why did you want to meet with me?

2. How did you get involved with Teach For America, and what kinds of things did you do in college?

3. From your experience in the corps and on staff, what have you seen as some of the most important skills for incoming corps members to have?

4. How accurate am I in my representation of Teach For America's mission, and how can I understand it better?

5. From talking to me, what do you consider my strengths in communicating to be, and where can I improve?

After your meeting, write down the most important issues that the RM talked about and think about how they relate to your own experiences. Think about how he represented himself and the organization, and make a plan for how you can incorporate these things into your application. Keep in mind that he will not be able to provide you with all of your answers, and you may come away with additional questions that he cannot answer. This meeting is simply a tool, just as this book and conversations with corps members, family, and friends, are tools to help you make the decision that is best for you.

Chapter 6

The Application Process

You should prepare for the application and interviews as thoroughly as possible, using both the guidelines in this book and those found on the Teach For America website. Taking the time to fully prepare will give you the best chance of being accepted. However, as you begin filling out the application, and as you walk into the interviews, my biggest advice is simply to do your best. It sounds cliché, but it is best to feel thoroughly prepared, stay relaxed, and not worry about hitting EVERY point. Otherwise, you will get distracted and will not be able to truly show the selection team who you are. Be yourself, be confident, and show them you are the leader they are looking for.

This chapter will be relatively short. The goal is to help you decide which deadline to choose and to outline the application process from beginning to end. I have set up the application timeline as a checklist so you can write in the dates for the deadline that you choose.

The following are Teach for America's minimum requirements for admission (for students graduating by spring 2013):

- Have a 2.5 undergraduate GPA

- Have a bachelor's degree by June 2013

- Be a U.S. citizen, national, or lawful permanent resident

If you have a GPA below 2.5, need one more class to graduate, or do not have one of the citizenship statuses mentioned above, you will not be allowed to apply and should pursue something else and/or wait until the following year to apply. The first two requirements are not set by Teach For America; they are minimum requirements set by the districts in which you will teach, and Teach For America has no say over them. The citizenship requirement stems from Teach For America's involvement with AmeriCorps, which is a governmental program that provides social services in the United States.

Which Deadline Should You Choose?

There are five deadlines by which you can apply.[1] Teach For America will tell you that it does not matter which deadline you choose and that you are just as likely to be accepted at the last deadline as the first one. I believe it to some degree; I do not think the program consciously favors early applicants over later ones. I do believe, though, that spaces fill up, and it can be more difficult to get accepted if you apply at the later deadlines, especially the final one. However, there are some important things you must consider when choosing a deadline, both from your perspective and from Teach For America's perspective.

First, it is helpful to know not only the date by which you must submit the initial application, but also the dates of the phone and final interviews. You will want to make sure, before all else, that there will not be any unavoidable conflicts during the phone and final interview weeks.

Also, recognize the benefits of applying early (i.e., one of the first three deadlines). Significantly fewer students apply early, so there will be more flexibility in terms of phone interview times, final interview times, and availability of the RM to talk you through any questions. In addition, you will know much earlier if you have been accepted, which will give you more time to prepare for the corps and to study for any tests that you must take to begin teaching. Getting accepted early will also eliminate all of the job-related stress you would otherwise experience in the spring. You will not have the pressure of building your leadership or getting straight As hanging over you in the fall semester. (I'm not saying that it's not important to keep your grades high for other reasons; they just won't impact your Teach For America application.) You will already know that you will be joining the corps and can enjoy the rest of your time in college.

---

1 Although the dates vary, the deadlines are usually in August, September, November, January, and February.

If you are absolutely certain that you want to join Teach For America, have done all of your research during your junior year in college (or have been out of college for one or more years), have spent extensive time getting to know your RM and current corps members, have significant leadership experience, and are ready to apply by the start of your senior year, you should apply at the earliest deadline possible. One additional perk is that regions and subjects may not have filled up yet, so if you are accepted, you may be more likely to be placed in the region and teach the subject you want. There are never any guarantees, and this should play into your decision less than the other benefits mentioned, but it is something to keep in mind.

There are also some downsides to applying early. By choosing one of the first three deadlines, you are effectively eliminating any achievements that you may gain during your senior year from your application. Senior year is often when students take on their most notable leadership roles. If you are expecting to receive a job promotion, be presented with an honor in your department, lead an event or trip for your organization, complete an honors thesis, or engage in a similarly impressive activity, you should think long and hard about waiting until those accomplishments are realized or more developed.

Applying to a later deadline allows all of those scenarios to play out and may help you present a much stronger application. If you are looking at other companies and organizations for a job post-graduation (which you should be), you will also prepare yourself by interviewing for those other positions before your Teach For America interviews. You will be just a little bit older and that much more experienced.

You may also form a better idea of where you want to be placed if you wait until later. It is nearly impossible to switch regions after acceptance, and there are any number of reasons why you may have one region in mind in August but a very different preference in January. For example, what if you are in a long-term relationship with a guy in Memphis in August but then break up with him in December? Memphis is a high-need region, so if you apply early and are accepted, you will likely get placed there. If you wait until the January deadline, though, you will know that you want to be in a different city; it may be the perfect opportunity to follow your dream of living in Los Angeles.

Finally, there may be logistical issues that determine a specific deadline preference. If you are studying abroad during the first semester of your senior year, you obviously should choose a later deadline so that you can attend a final interview if selected. Alternately, if you are going to be spending your final semester interning full-time in Washington, D.C., you should choose a deadline during the first semester, unless you think you can afford to spend the time and energy needed to apply during the internship.

To recap, here are the pros and cons of applying early and applying late. In the end, your decision is entirely up to you, and there is no right or wrong decision. You should choose a deadline that works best with your schedule and one that will allow you to best present yourself. If possible, however, I would advise against applying at the final deadline. It is by far the most popular deadline and may inhibit your ability to get accepted to the region that you would like.

Applying Early (first three deadlines)

Pros:

- Know earlier whether you get accepted and where you are placed if you do

- Have more time to prepare for the corps and study for any required tests

- More flexibility in choosing interview times and dates

- Greater availability to speak with the RM about Teach For America and your application

- Possibly more likely to receive your most preferred region and subject placements

Cons:

- Any accomplishments or honors during your senior year are irrelevant

- Less time to leverage your experiences into leadership positions

- Less time to gain experience interviewing with other organizations and companies
- Have to decide whether to accept before you have other options
- Potentially less time to research Teach For America if you have not been proactive

Applying Late (final two deadlines)

Pros:

- Better opportunity to gain leadership positions that you can use in your application
- Opportunity to improve your GPA, if needed
- Better idea of what locations and subject areas you prefer
- More time to research Teach For America if you were not interested early
- More time to build a relationship with the RM

Cons:

- Less flexibility in choosing interview times and dates
- Less opportunity to be in constant communication with your RM during the application process
- Know much later if you are accepted, possibly leading to stress if you have no other options
- If your high-target region fills up, you will not be placed where you want to be
- Less time to study for certification tests (failing a test in the summer before the school year begins may inhibit your ability to be hired in your school district)

Timeline

Here is the application process from start to finish. I have formatted this section as a checklist so that you can keep track of where you are in the process. I have also included a space next to each step for you to write in the dates for the application deadline you choose.

_____**Step 1: Submit your application.** The application can be found on the Teach For America website by going to www.teachforamerica.org and clicking "Apply to the Corps." The application is due by 11:59 p.m. on the deadline listed.

_____**Step 2:** Teach For America will tell you if you have been invited to an interview or if you have not made the cut. You will be notified both by email and on your Teach For America status page after 6:00 p.m. (eastern time) on the date listed for your deadline.

_____**Step 3:** If you are invited to continue to either the phone interview or the final interview, you will need to complete an online activity. The activity will be available for approximately one week and MUST be completed in one sitting. This will involve pre-reading, and it may take up to two hours, so plan accordingly.

_____**Step 4:** Provide Teach For America with contact information for two recommenders and one reference, called the Recommenders/Reference List (RRL). There is a clear difference between your recommenders and reference, which I will explain in Chapter 8, but you should start thinking now about the three people who know you best in a professional, academic, or extracurricular capacity.

_____Step 5: Phone interview. The phone interview is scheduled in half-hour increments, but there is a chance it could go longer. You should block out an hour of time when scheduling your phone interview just to be safe.

_____Step 6: Assignment Preference Form (APF) and Coursework Information Form (CIF). If you are invited to advance to the final interview, you will fill out these two forms online. The APF is the form on which you officially rank your preferences for region, subject, and grade level placement. On the CIF, you will input additional information that Teach For America will use to determine what you are qualified to teach, if accepted.

_____Step 7: Final interview. The final interview is a full-day group interview consisting of 7–12 applicants and a variety of activities and interviews. You must be able to attend a final interview in person, and you should plan to be there for the entire working day (8:00 a.m.–5:00 p.m.). Make sure you do not have any work, school, or volunteer conflicts on the day that you choose.

_____Step 8: Notification of final status. You will be notified by a specified date if you have been accepted into the corps. You will have approximately two weeks to decide if you want to accept or decline. During this time, representatives from Teach For America will reach out to you to answer any questions and respond to any concerns you may have.

For the remainder of the book, I will be explaining each of these steps in more detail, both from a logistical and a strategic perspective. As we discuss each step in the process, you should refer back to the ideas from the first part of the book to present yourself in the best possible light.

Chapter 7

The Application

You have internalized Teach For America's mission and spent time discussing it with your family and friends. You are able to express your experiences in a quantitative way that effectively portrays those qualities that the organization seeks in applicants. You are keeping your grades up and have found ways to get more actively involved in leadership roles with your associations. You have revamped your online presence and spoken with the RM and local corps members. You have decided that becoming a corps member is the right next step for you. It is now time to apply to Teach For America.

There are four parts to the application:

- Prerequisites

- Personal Information

- Academic History

- Leadership Experience

Starting the Application

Go to the Teach For America website and click "Start a New Application." At the beginning, Teach For America will ask you a number of questions about your education and leadership background. Answer each of them to the best of your ability, including your career sector and your leadership role. If you have already graduated, your career sector should be the industry in which you currently work; otherwise, choose your student status from the list ("Full Time Undergraduate Student," for example). When deciding what to list as your leadership role, choose one that exemplifies your management of others and one in which you have had significant and quantifiable results. This could be your position in student government, your role at a company, or any other impressive responsibility. You will have plenty of time to expand on the role you choose later in the application.

Once you begin your application, you will open what is called the "Applicant Center." It is here that you will submit everything required for your application, including additional documents if you are invited to the phone and final interview rounds, and where all communication with Teach For America regarding your application and admission decision will occur.

Prerequisites

These are the first two pages of the application. You must confirm that you are a U.S. citizen, national, or lawful resident, that you have a high school degree or equivalent, that you will have above a 2.5 GPA by the time you graduate, and that you will graduate by June of the year in which you apply.

You will then select a deadline; doing this will generate all of the crucial dates for the application process. Once you select your deadline, go back to the timeline in Chapter 6 and write in the dates given to you.

Finally, you will choose three locations for your final interview, should you advance to that round. Be sure to check your calendar to avoid future conflicts. Choose locations to which you can travel easily. Make sure that your first selection is most convenient for you and that you will be able to attend if you reach the final interview. If no other choices are convenient, feel free to mark them as "Less Convenient." If you foresee transportation problems due to long distance, start making plans now to borrow a car or take a train or a bus.

Personal Information

This is the first real page of the application. This page asks for your basic contact information, information about your hometown, and your letter of intent. The contact information part of this page is relatively straightforward. The letter of intent, however, is one of the major sections of your application, and you should spend a significant amount of time writing and perfecting it.

Letter of Intent

Think of the letter of intent as a structured cover letter: It gives you an opportunity to go beyond your resume and present your experiences and goals in a way that helps you stand out. Spend a lot of time thinking about what the questions mean to you, creating an outline, and putting your heart and soul into writing it. If you prepare well and put passion into your response, the reader will clearly be able to tell that you took the time to think deeply about the questions.

The letter of intent has three parts and a maximum limit of 500 words, less than one single-spaced page in Microsoft Word. You don't have a lot of room, so make your response clear, concise, and compelling. You must have an excellent writing style, including strong paragraph structure and correct grammar. Make sure your answers flow together in a meaningful way. Also, remember that this is *one* letter of intent—not three distinct, short-answer paragraphs—so your letter should be structured and formatted as a single, continuous piece of writing.

I am not going to spend this section telling you what to write. Your answers must come from within and reflect well on you; otherwise, the selection team will quickly figure out that you are not truly invested in the program. What I can tell you, though, is how to think about the questions in order to answer them effectively.[1]

Prompt

In 500 words, answer the following questions in a well-thought-out, thorough letter of intent:

1. Why do you seek to join Teach For America?

2. What would you hope to accomplish as a corps member?

3. How would you determine your success as a corps member?

---

1   To read a sample letter of intent, refer to Appendix 2.

Why Do You Seek to Join Teach For America?

By this point, you should already have your answer to this question in your head; it is now just a matter of putting it down on paper. Think about the top two or three reasons that have motivated you to spend the time learning about Teach For America, talking to corps members and recruiters, and working on the application. Is it your desire to provide for others the same education as you had received? Is it your passion for education or social reform? Was it your conversation or interaction with a kid that really opened your eyes to the extreme injustices in our nation? There are a thousand reasons why someone would want to join this movement. As long as your intentions are honest, there are no wrong answers.

Your response should be meaningful to you and should shout enthusiasm and passion. A short anecdote can be a great way to add a little life and personality to your response. If you have many reasons for applying, focus on one or two of the most important ones, or try to tell a story that encapsulates them all. Your reason should NOT be, "I don't know what I want to do, so I want to spend two years with Teach For America figuring it out and building my resume."

When I wrote my letter of intent, I cited the education I had received as the principal reason I wanted to join Teach For America. I attended a public school in the Cincinnati School District, which, at the time, was the lowest-performing school district in Ohio. Yet, my school, Walnut Hills High School, was consistently ranked in the top 40 nationwide in *Newsweek* rankings and offered more AP classes than any other school in the nation. At graduation, we had students from million-dollar households standing shoulder to shoulder with students from welfare families. Ninety-nine percent of my graduating class attended college. Walnut Hills is what education can and should be, and it inspired me to help shape that reality in the highest-need schools in our country.

What Do You Hope to Accomplish as a Corps Member?

I find this question interesting because of the wide array of goals an applicant can have. Should you talk about what you hope to accomplish with individual students, within your school placement, or your own personal growth? Should you talk about tangible results you hope to achieve in the classroom or about more "macro" ideas of closing the achievement gap in our country? You can really choose any of these directions, so decide what it is that you really hope to accomplish. Be realistic with your expectations. You will not single-handedly close the achievement gap in New York City, but you might double a student's reading growth each year you are his teacher. This is also a good place to reference Teach For America's mission and values to show that you have put in the time and effort to internalize them.

Regardless of your answer, include your potential future students in your response to at least some degree. Remember, the only reason Teach For America exists is to improve the education of students, so this must be a key element of your response. Talk about the specific gains you hope to see in your kids, the ways you want to help your students think critically, or some other measure of student success. At the same time, keep in mind that a large part of Teach For America's mission revolves around developing future leaders. Discussing personal development and the leadership skills you hope to gain is not a sign of selfishness or heady ambition, especially if you emphasize the way you hope to use those skills in your career to make a difference. It shows that you are thinking critically about the skills Teach For America will help you gain and the ways you will give back when you finish your commitment.

How Would You Determine Your Success as a Corps Member?

I hope by now you have a sense of how Teach For America measures success. Quantitative results are essential, and analyzing test scores, subject mastery percentages, and attendance rates for your students will be a huge part of what you do every day. Just as you have quantified your own successes in the application, make sure to use numbers when defining success. Does "success" mean that the average mastery in your classes will be at least 80 percent? Does it mean that your elementary students will increase their reading levels by an average of 1.5 years? While you may not have thought about your own successes in this manner when you were in school, you had some standard you were expected to achieve. Plan to hold your students to that same high standard.

That being said, Teach For America is starting to include some qualitative assessments in its tracking and measurement system, so if you have some creative and innovative ways to recognize success, both inside and outside of the classroom, discuss those ideas here. In addition to high grades and test scores, strong attendance rates, and excellence in challenging classes, think deeper about other ways you felt successful as a student and why that success happened. Was it a teacher's calm but consistently firm demeanor or her ability to make the information fun? Was it the fact that you felt safe to speak out in class without fear of embarrassment? Think about why those things happened and how you might be able to duplicate them in your own classroom. A little creativity, on top of the quantitative objectives, will help you stand out.

Teach For America suggests using an online program called ETS Proofreader to electronically proofread your letter. While it is not a bad way to get instant feedback, it is certainly not as effective as having someone else review it (plus, you have to pay a small fee for the service). My advice is to show your essay to as many trustworthy people as possible for feedback and proofreading. Take it to the campus writing lab if your college has one. Refine your essay over and over, until it is as engaging, compelling, and concise as you can make it.

A piece of advice when asking others for feedback: People are inherently non-confrontational and will avoid saying things so as not to hurt your feelings. If you tell them upfront that you welcome constructive criticism and that they should not hold back, you will get much more meaningful responses from them.

A well-structured letter of intent will flow smoothly, be free of punctuation and spelling mistakes, and have varied sentence structure and strong transitions. Remember, most of the readers were teachers at some point, and teachers are notorious for finding even the smallest writing mistakes. Also, make sure that you thoroughly address all three questions in your letter. You do not want to write a separate answer for each of the three; you want to create a comprehensive response to the questions as a whole.

Academic History

This page asks you to list some detailed information about your academic achievements. First, you will need to know your cumulative GPA, as well as yearly GPAs from your undergraduate education. If you are still in college, download an unofficial transcript or request one from the university. Usually, these are free to download and print. If you are out of college, you should request an unofficial transcript from your university or find out if you can access it online.

Enter the information exactly as it appears on your transcript. Do NOT fudge your information or lie about your grades; you will be sending Teach For America an official copy of your transcript if you are invited to the final interview. In addition to your cumulative GPA, Teach For America requests your GPA for each year. Because your transcript likely does not calculate this for you, Teach For America provides you with a calculator to obtain these numbers. For each year, enter the grades you received for that year and click "calculate" to get that year's GPA.

Teach For America will then ask a number of additional questions about your academic career. Answer all required questions honestly, even if you think they may hurt your application, as you will have an opportunity to explain any deficiencies.

Some of the questions are optional, but I recommend answering them if they help shed a positive light on your candidacy. For example, one of the optional questions asks about your work experience during college. As mentioned earlier, working to finance your tuition shows great leadership potential, and even if you only worked part-time for spending money, you should enter that information.

Leadership Experience

On this page, you will be asked to both upload your resume and enter information about extracurricular, volunteer, and professional activities in which you were engaged as an undergraduate or graduate student. Formatting your resume and entering your activities will both take some time, so just as with your letter of intent, be sure to get started well ahead of the deadline.

Once you upload your resume, you will need to answer several additional questions. These questions are very self-explanatory, so answer them to the best of your ability. The first question, however, is the only one on the application for which I can almost definitively tell you what answer to select. It asks if you have ever held a leadership role in any activity. Click "Yes," unless you *really* have not had any semblance of a leadership role. By now, the importance of leadership to Teach For America should be clear, and you should already have been thinking about how to present your credentials as a leader. If you answer "No," any future discussion of leadership is undermined.

Resume

A resume is essentially a one-page snapshot of your professional accomplishments. It is inherently formulaic, so it can be difficult to differentiate yourself. I would recommend consulting all available resources to help you create the strongest resume possible. There are hundreds of websites that will help you develop it, and your college career center, or equivalent, likely has a lab that will critique your resume, edit your formatting, and help create catchy, professional descriptions of your experiences. During this process, though, keep in mind that the recommendations below are specific to Teach For America. These tips may not be true for all jobs that you apply for.

Resume Overview

When discussing the resume, I will refer to what I call "resume blocks." A resume block is simply one position or accomplishment followed by supporting details and bullets. The look of resume blocks can vary, depending on the heading and information needed (we'll look at a few examples later).

First and foremost, remember that Teach For America wants to see ambitious, measurable results. As Teach For America is big on numbers and data, selectors will expect to see that represented in your resume. Do not be vague about your accomplishments. Clearly explain your specific roles and the results you obtained. You should vary your action words and keep the descriptions simple and straightforward.

Nothing is worse than reading a resume with confusing, wordy descriptions that could be stated much more clearly and concisely. You don't need to impress the resume reader with big words. If the reader can't understand your descriptions through a quick skim of your resume, she likely won't read it at all. To illustrate this, consider these two descriptions of a fundraising accomplishment:

- "Oversaw team of 15 fundraisers in outreach, coordination, and planning of annual event that raised $27,548 (+17% from previous year)"

- "Oversaw 15 highly motivated team members in developing and coordinating the annual fundraising event for outreach to high potential donors, coordination of all event logistics, and all subsequent planning, leading to a fundraising net gain of $27,548, an increase of 17% over the previous year's totals"

There is nothing in the second description that is not in the first. The only difference between the two is that the first one is written much more concisely, and is thus more effective. I like to keep all of my descriptions to one line, although I have seen great resumes with two-line descriptions. Any more than two lines and you risk becoming unfocused and wordy. Keep it simple.

Formatting

Keep your formatting consistent throughout your resume. Use the same font throughout, the same size and styles for all headlines, and the same bullet style for your descriptions. If possible, use the same number of bullets for each description. Your name should be the only text bigger than size 14 font.

I would recommend using a standard font like Arial or Helvetica. Your name should be in size 20–24 font, and the rest of the resume should be in either size 11 or 12. You can use bolding and italics to highlight certain types of information; just make sure you stay consistent. For example, if you italicize the dates of your most recent job, italicize all dates on the resume.

One final note: The human eye is pleased by empty space, so try to create some white areas in your resume to make it more aesthetically pleasing and readable.

Resume Sections

Your resume should include the sections listed below. Depending on your personal accomplishments, some of these sections may be more or less important, or can be left out entirely. You may also include additional sections if your background is especially unique or specific.[2]

Header

Your full name should be at the top in big font, size 20 or bigger. Underneath, in normally sized font, include your current address, cell phone number, and email address. Please, please, *please* make sure that your email address is something like firstname.lastname@college.edu instead of whosyadaddy@gmail.com. I see unprofessional emails all the time on resumes. If you don't have a professional address, get one. You are about to leave college or out of college already, and important people don't want to feel like they are communicating with a 13-year-old.

Education

List your education in reverse chronological order. For each of your schools, include your degree, major(s) and minor(s), GPA (include your major GPA separately if it is higher than your cumulative GPA), and all honors, accomplishments, awards, honors theses, etc. This includes things like dean's list mentions, departmental honors, and student awards. If you studied abroad, you should indicate that as well. Unless your study abroad experience exemplifies real and outstanding leadership, just include it in your undergrad block.

Leadership Experience and Work Experience

Decide which category is more compelling and significant and list that one first. As a junior or senior in college, your leadership experience may very well be more significant than your work experience. If you

2 To see an example of an exemplary resume, refer to Appendix 3.

are out of college and have been working for a few years, your work experience is likely more important.

Try to keep all of the resume blocks in these two sections consistent in terms of number of bullets per block and styles for company names, positions, and dates. You should use three bullets in each of these blocks. If you have too many experiences and your resume is more than one page, you can cut the number of bullets to two in each block of the less significant category to fit everything on one page.

I have a specific structure that I like to use, but there are countless other formats out there. Take mine if you would like, or modify it in a way that suits you. This is the format I use for all of my resume blocks in the Leadership Experience and Work Experience categories:

Company or Organization, *Position Title* – City, State   *Date Started - Date Ended (or "- Present" if still there)*

One-line explanatory phrase about the company, general description of the position, or any other general content you want to include

- Most significant responsibility or accomplishment, described using quantitative data
- Next most significant responsibility or accomplishment, described using quantitative data if possible
- Next most significant responsibility or accomplishment, described using quantitative data (in some cases, you may only use 2 bullets)

Remember the college newspaper editor from Chapter 3? Let's create two possible resume blocks for her position. Once again, try to figure out which one is more effective in revealing all of her leadership qualities and accomplishments.

XYZ University Newspaper, *Editor-in-Chief* – Boston, MA   *Sept. 2011 - Present*

- Responsible for overseeing all news and editorial content
- Facilitate communication between page editors, reconcile all disagreements, and final decision maker on page content
- Responsible for determining, allocating, dispersing, and substantiating page budgets to page editors and their respective contingents from an umbrella budget
- Increased circulation of the newspaper in 2011 by placing additional newsstands downtown

XYZ University Newspaper, *Editor-in-Chief* – Boston, MA   *Sept. 2011 - Present*

XYZ University Newspaper is a daily student-run newspaper representing student, local, and national issues at XYZ University

- Administer a yearly budget of $1,800,000; responsible for determining and allocating funds to 9 page editors quarterly
- Manage 20 page editors, reporters, and photographers, including assigning deadlines and facilitating communication
- Lobbied City Council to allow XYZ to place newsstands downtown, increasing circulation from 20,000 to 33,000 readers (65% growth)

Hopefully you selected the second example, which presents the editor's accomplishments in a quantitative, easily understood way. It is well organized; she starts off with a description of the newspaper and follows it with three outstanding examples of her leadership. She uses enough words to explain the accomplishments and no more. Every word has a purpose.

The first block, on the other hand, is unorganized, and the listed accomplishments are not measurable. The editor is vague in some places and excessively wordy in others. She has no description of the paper, which would likely be more of a problem for a less common or understood position. We can see that she is accomplished, but we don't know to what extent. She is leaving out the most important details— that she managed nearly $2 million and 20 people, while increasing circulation by 65 percent.

Leadership Experience

Your leadership experience consists of anything you have done in extracurricular and volunteer positions. If you started a nonprofit or a campus organization, list it under Leadership Experience. Paid positions can also be listed if the experience itself was more important or significant than the money you earned. Use strong action words and define your accomplishments in measurable and meaningful ways.

Work Experience

Your work experience should include positions where you were directly employed or where you started your own company. The formatting for your work experience should be exactly the same as that of your leadership experience. Use a descriptive tag for your company or position and then add bullets with specific examples of leadership. Again, describe your positions in ways that demonstrate leadership in quantifiable terms.

Additional Information/Skills/Honors

Here, you should list all technical skills, languages spoken, and non-academic honors you have received. You can also list personal skills or interests if they are important parts of who you are. Don't go overboard with them, but if you are a classical cellist and have been playing since you were five years old, you may stick out if you mention it.

Extracurricular and Professional Pursuits

In addition to providing your resume, you will need to give detailed explanations of two to four extracurricular activities or work engagements with which you were involved as an undergraduate or graduate student. This is your opportunity to expand on at least two of the leadership positions you listed on your resume, especially if you were not able to describe the full breadth of your positions due to space constraints. These should be the most significant jobs you held or groups you were involved with in college. Ideally, pick engagements in which you held the highest positions and the most responsibility, because those roles give the best representation of your ability to lead others and achieve success in your endeavors.

Be honest when entering descriptions of your roles, but be sure not to diminish your accomplishments. In addition to entering basic information about each position, such as type of organization and number of members or employees, you will be asked to write brief explanations of your responsibilities and contributions in the role. It is important to present the quantitative results you obtained and the leadership positions you held. Discuss the number of people you managed or led, the amount of money you raised, the number of people you supported, and any other impressive accomplishments. Take full advantage of the space; there is no word limit. While you shouldn't write a novel, you should use the space to describe every responsibility and impressive contribution you made.

Make sure that your entries are grammatically correct. While it is less important to structure these explanations formally, as you did in the letter of intent, readers will certainly notice rushed responses, spelling errors, and weak grammar. Review your entries and show them to at least one other person to catch errors you may have missed.

Teach For America provides further explanations and guidelines to help you complete each part of this section. Read each explanation carefully and, where appropriate, try to construct your answers in a similar fashion as the examples given. Most importantly, remember that it is essential to describe quantitative results that portray exceptional outcomes.[3]

Review and Submit

Review your application multiple times before you submit it. This includes everything from making sure your email address is typed correctly to proofreading your letter of intent. Once you submit your application, you cannot go back and edit it. Be sure that you have included every piece of information you want Teach For America to see and that you have crafted the strongest application possible.

When you are ready to send in your application, hit "Submit." You will know that you have successfully submitted the application when you are redirected to a page that lists the time when your application was submitted AND you receive a confirmation email.

---

3 For an example of how to enter an extracurricular activity, refer to Appendix 4.

Chapter 8

Online Activity and Recommenders/Reference List

Online Activity

If you are invited to continue to the phone interview or are advanced directly to the final interview (which a small percentage of applicants are), you will be asked to read a few articles and complete an online activity in the Applicant Center. You will have access to the activity for approximately one week after you are invited to begin. It is important to note that you must complete the activity in one sitting; you cannot start it and then come back to it later. You will need Internet access and either headphones or speakers to listen to the audio portions of the activity.

My advice is to block off at least two hours to complete this activity with absolutely no distractions. Find a place with reliable Internet access where you know you will not be sidetracked by anyone or anything. If you are going to complete it in your bedroom, lock your door and tell any roommates that you cannot be interrupted until you come out. If you are going to use the library, find an area that is not crowded so that you will not see your friends or be otherwise distracted. If you are going to a coffee shop, pick one with good Internet and away from campus, where you will be less likely to run into friends.

The activity consists of both multiple-choice and free-response questions. Take your time, as this will be used in the final evaluation of your candidacy. The activity will ask you to discuss your interest in and understanding of Teach For America, as well as test your ability to solve problems and reach conclusions by working through data. Before you begin, print out the articles provided, read them carefully, and take notes directly on the pages. Although the activity will not directly test your comprehension of the articles, reading them ahead of time will help you reflect on the issues presented in the activity. This exercise is not exceptionally hard, but it is not to be taken lightly either.

Recommenders/Reference List

You will also need to provide contact information for two recommenders and one reference. For many applicants, this is actually the most difficult part of the application process, and it can be a key factor in their admittance or rejection. It is very important to find people who worked with you recently and know your work very well. Do not use your supervisor from eight years ago, your father's friend in the U.S. Senate whom you have never met, or a professor you have known for three weeks. Teach For America knows that people prioritize their time differently, so you will not lose points if your recommenders are not highly influential people. The organization just wants to hear from the people who know your work best. They should be able to advocate for you to the highest degree.

Recommenders

Teach For America states that recommenders can be drawn from any of three contexts:

- Professional: manager, supervisor, director, internship coordinator
- Academic: professor, thesis advisor, independent research advisor
- Extracurricular: coach, director, advisor

You should start preparing to ask for letters of recommendation 6–12 months before you apply. You should be going out of your way to introduce yourself to your bosses, professors, and other people of influence. Ask a professor if you can work directly under her to do research or help with experiments. If you know that one of your professors is writing a book, ask if he needs assistance. If you volunteer for an organization, make sure you get to know your direct supervisor well. All of this should be done so they can write informed recommendations for you when the time comes. As someone who has written recommendation letters for both students and colleagues, I cannot emphasize enough how important it is to know the recommender well.

You are required to submit contact information for two different recommenders, each of whom will fill out a recommendation form provided online by Teach For America. Again, they should know you well and be strong advocates for you; they should know your strengths and weaknesses and be able to talk confidently about what you would bring to the classroom as a corps member. It will be helpful if they know your career aspirations.

Your recommenders should also know about Teach For America and its mission. If they do not, find a time to talk to them about Teach For America and why you are interested in joining the program. By this point, you should have internalized Teach For America's mission and be prepared to talk to others about it. Educating your recommenders on this point will also be great practice for the phone and final interviews. Finally, you should impress upon them the importance of the recommendation form.

If you are still in college, my advice is to make one of your recommenders a professor who is very familiar with your academic work. While Teach For America will not weight a professor above a different position as a recommender, the most significant experience that you have had in college is your educational career, so you should try to have somebody representing you well from that area. For your other recommendation, pick someone from your professional life or from an extracurricular or volunteer activity. You don't necessarily *have* to choose a professor if you know two outstanding people from work and extracurricular experience, but try not to select two recommenders from the same field. You want the recommendations to complement each other by describing different skill sets, providing a well-rounded picture of who you are.

Give your recommenders plenty of time to complete the letters. Before you even apply, you should reach out to potential recommenders to let them know that you may soon ask them to fill out a recommendation form. They need to know that this is not a standard letter of recommendation, but a specific form that Teach For America will send them via email. They must be comfortable using the Internet and submitting information online.

The day that you know you have moved on to the final interview round and will need recommendations, you should contact them to remind them to look out for an email from Teach For America. In your email, thank them for taking the time to write the letter, emphasize the deadline, and ask them to let you know when they have completed the recommendation. If they do not already have a copy of your resume, send that to them as well. If you are approaching the deadline and they have not yet submitted the recommendation form, send a friendly reminder with the deadline highlighted. You can always find out where your recommenders are in the process by logging into the Applicant Center.

Reference

You are also required to submit contact information for a third individual, a reference. She may or may not be contacted, but should know you well and should be able to speak about you in one of the three contexts mentioned above. She will not be required to submit an online form; if selectors feel they need additional information about your background, someone from Teach For America will contact her by phone or email. You have the option of choosing one of your recommenders as your reference, but I highly advise against that (as does Teach For America).

Your reference should by no means be weaker than your recommenders simply because she may or may not be contacted. She can represent the third field not covered by the two recommenders, although she does not have to. Most importantly, she should be an additional advocate who knows you and your skill sets very well. The selection team is not shy about calling references. If Teach For America decides it needs this one more piece of information about you, then your reference may single-handedly determine whether you are accepted or not.

Chapter 9

The Phone Interview

If you impress Teach For America with your application, you will either be invited to participate in a phone interview or advance directly to the final interview. (Even if you are invited to skip the phone interview, you should still read this chapter, as there is good interview preparation advice here.) The phone interview will last about 30 minutes. Your interviewer will ask questions about your resume, your knowledge of Teach For America and the education movement, your organizational skills, and any number of other topics. You should stay calm and answer the questions as clearly and concisely as possible.

Because so many applicants are invited to participate in the phone interview, your interviewer will likely be a current corps member, a regional staff member, or an alumnus/a. Try not to be too nervous or intimidated; interviewing is definitely not your interviewer's full-time job. Because phone interviews are standardized across the country, the questions may feel a bit scripted and the conversation might not flow as naturally as you would like. Your interviewer will probably warn you about this, but just be aware that there may be extended pauses after your responses while the interviewer finishes taking notes. This is no cause for panic.

> "Be honest during your interviews, especially in regard to your personal understanding of what being a TFA corps member entails (i.e., hard work, lots of days that you are frustrated and think are fruitless, schools without management systems, etc.). I remember being candid in my interviews and saying that of course there would be days when I was going to struggle in my job and not want to get up in the morning, but that the purpose of helping children was so important that everything

> *in comparison was well worth the effort. I think being cognizant of these issues but still being passionate about wanting to make a difference resonated during my interviews, and eventually helped me during my two years teaching."*
>
> —Devin Potts (Philadelphia '09)

How to Prepare

You will likely be asked to elaborate on your resume and letter of intent by talking through some of your most impressive leadership experiences. You may also be asked to talk about the articles you read in preparation for the online activity. The interviewer might ask you to offer an opinion on an article, suggest a solution to a problem discussed in an article, or just summarize the argument of one of the authors. Make sure that you have not only read the articles, but also developed an opinion on them ahead of time so that you can speak intelligently on the issues.

Apart from questions about the articles, you generally will answer the same types of questions as you would in a standard job interview. Answer them honestly and to the best of your ability. Stay confident and be concise, and speak about your quantitative accomplishments just as you did in your resume and your letter of intent.

While there is no way to predict the actual interview, you should prepare responses to the following questions:

- Why do you want to join Teach for America?
- What is the most difficult situation that you have had to handle?
- What is your most significant accomplishment?
- Have you ever missed a deadline?
- Tell me about yourself.

Once you have finished developing answers, have a friend or family member call you and practice the questions over the phone. Communicating by phone can be tricky compared to doing so in person, so this is a great way to get in the rhythm of a phone conversation.

You should also prepare three questions to ask the interviewer at the end of the interview. Good questions will address the interviewer's experience in the corps, how he likes being a corps member, or the biggest difficulty he faces or faced every day as a teacher. You can also ask any logistical questions about Teach For America to which you have not yet found the answer. As a side note, I would shy away from asking questions that are too off-the-wall and avoid questions of a political or socioeconomic nature. It would be a shame to get docked in the respect column because you asked a question the interviewer deemed offensive.

The Interview

When scheduling your phone interview time, think of when and where you will have a place that is quiet and free from distractions. Unlike the online activity, for which a library or coffee shop will suffice, you need to be able to talk comfortably without background noise. You should also be at a table or desk, so you can lay out information to reference throughout the call. Some good options are your room (if you live in a quiet house), your parents' house (if you live close to home), an empty classroom on campus, a soundproof study room in the library, or the apartment of a friend who lives alone. Bad options are coffee shops (either too quiet to talk or too loud to hear), your living room (if you have roommates), common rooms in a dorm (too many distractions), your car (no desk, and it will get unbearably hot or cold, depending on the season), and anywhere outside (too many distractions and background noises).

Start preparing yourself one hour before the interview begins. Begin with a desk or table free of clutter. If you are in your room, clear off everything from your desk that does not have to do with Teach For America. On the table, you should lay out:

1. Your resume, with important blocks highlighted and notes for yourself to reference if they are not in the resume

2. Your letter of intent, with specific parts highlighted to remind you of important details

3. The articles given to you to read, with notes jotted down in the margins and/or important parts highlighted

4. Your summary and overall response and opinion of each article, preferably typed and printed so they are easy to read

5. Note cards with any other important information that you have not mentioned anywhere else in your application but would like to talk about if the opportunity arises

6. Questions you want to ask the interviewer when he is done asking you questions

7. Any other materials you think might help you in the interview, such as outlines to expected questions to remind you of talking points

Arrange these pieces of information in a way that is logical to you and that will allow you to find information quickly and easily. You want this setup to be helpful, not distracting. Practice referring to certain pages based on different questions that may be asked of you. The interview most likely will not follow the path you anticipated at all, but at least you will be comfortable with the location of the various resources.

My most potent advice is to be comfortable, confident, and honest. You have made it this far, which means Teach For America has rated your application as stronger than that of tens of thousands of other applicants. Candid, passionate, concise, and quantitative responses will get you to the final interview.

Chapter 10

Choosing Regions, Subjects, and Grade Level

If you are invited to advance to the final interview, you will be asked to go to the Applicant Center and complete the Assignment Preference Form (APF), which tells Teach For America the regions, subjects, and grades you are interested in teaching, and the Coursework Information Form (CIF), which allows the organization to determine what you are qualified to teach. These are the official forms that Teach For America will use to decide where you are placed and what you will teach if you are accepted. Teach For America carefully takes these preferences into account; the organization knows that you are much more likely to accept the offer if you are given the region, subject, and grade level that you want.

These selections have absolutely no bearing on your admission to Teach For America. The selection team does not even look at a candidate's preferences until they have made the final decision on whether or not you are accepted. However, in some situations, applicants are placed on a wait list, and this is when your selections may come into play. Applicants are put on the wait list if Teach For America believes they are a strong fit for the program, but there are no openings available for them. While you should not make your decisions with the off-chance that it will influence your placement on the wait list, choosing a broader range of regions and content areas may increase the likelihood that you will be offered a position immediately, instead of being wait-listed.

If you are placed on the wait list, the organization has decided that you have the leadership potential to be a great corps member, but there are simply not enough spaces nationally to place you at that time. If situations change and they find a space for you, then you will be accepted into the corps. If you are placed on the wait list, you will have the opportunity to revise your choices in terms of region, subject, and grade level. If you are set on joining Teach For America, I recommend considering broadening your choices to include ones that you did not select the first time.

This also reinforces one of the benefits of applying early: There are more openings available in terms of region and subject preferences. Certain regions and subjects are more popular than others, and the fact is, there is a limit to the number of teachers needed in any given region. While there is never any guarantee, if you are dead-set on a certain city or content area, you should apply early to give yourself the greatest opportunity to receive your preference.

When picking regions, you will see a list of all 46 regions in which Teach For America operates.[1] Applicants must choose at least 10 of the regions and assign them to one of three categories: highly preferred, preferred, or least preferred. Within each category, you can further rank your choices in the order of preference, and can even choose to rank regions at the same level within each category. For example, when I applied, my rankings looked like this:

Highly Preferred	Preferred	Least Preferred
1. Chicago	1. Los Angeles	1. Boston
1. Philadelphia	2. Hawaii	2. New York City
2. San Francisco	2. Newark	3. St. Louis
2. Washington, D.C.	3. Greater New Orleans	4. Baltimore

My rankings look slightly different than yours will because Teach For America now requires all applicants to rank at least one priority region in the highly preferred, preferred, or least preferred category. Although the regions labeled as priority change each year based on need, some past examples of priority regions are Detroit, Memphis, Oklahoma, New Mexico, and Mississippi Delta. This system was not in place when I applied.

---

1 Teach For America has placed corps members in 46 regions at the time of writing.

You will then rank all subjects and grade levels as highly preferred, preferred, or least preferred, much like you did when selecting regions. Math and science teachers are in high demand, and if you are interested in teaching, say, high school biology, you will have a strong chance of getting that placement. Elementary education is a little more competitive, and generally less needed, so you may end up teaching a completely different grade level if you select elementary. Understand, though, that ultimately there is no guarantee that you will get what you want in any of these categories. I have friends who listed middle school and math as highly preferred, and listed Philadelphia as the least preferred region, and they ended up teaching high school Spanish in Philadelphia.

Do not list regions where you definitely would not go on your APF, and do not list grade levels and subjects you would not teach as highly preferred or preferred, with the hope that Teach For America will take into account your flexibility in deciding whether or not to admit you. The APF is the only way Teach For America knows your preferences, so it is very important to think carefully about what you would and would not accept as a placement. It is perfectly fine to choose regions and subjects that you highly prefer to teach and avoid those that you definitely would not accept.

Although there are no guarantees, some selections do seem to be better guaranteed than others. If you list a priority region as your absolute number one choice, you will likely be placed in that region. If you select high school math or science, as long as you are qualified to teach it according to your CIF, you will probably get it because those spots are harder for low-income schools to fill. If you rank special education as highly preferred or even preferred, there is a very good chance you will receive that placement. These spots are simply harder to fill through traditional selection and are where Teach For America teachers are often needed most.

In the end, you are signing up to serve for two years and work in a very difficult environment. Teach For America will not be easy, and you should not expect it to be. Be open to exploring opportunities outside of what you originally had in mind. Choosing to go to the Mississippi Delta may not be your first choice, but there are a lot of passionate people working hard in the priority regions. I have heard time and time again that corps members in the highest-need regions are among the most thrilled with their Teach For America experience because they feel like they are truly at the center of the reform movement.

Chapter 11

The Final Interview

Relax. The final interview day is fun. The interviewers will do everything they can to put your mind at ease. They are not intimidating; many of them have only been out of the corps for a year or two. They are simply there to find the best people to enter the classroom next fall. Just by being in that room, you have already advanced further than the vast majority of applicants, so you should go in confident and focused. You know that your application and phone interview (if you had one) were strong enough that Teach For America decided you are worth spending a full day interviewing. You do not have to try to act like someone you are not. Stay calm, confident, and enjoy the experience.

Preparing for the Final Interview

I called my parents as soon as TFA offered me the daylong interview. I had never interviewed while applying for a job or to college; this was my first one. My mother was quick to both share her excitement and her nerves. After speaking with her at length, I became determined to be the most prepared person in my interview group.

I found the TFA website helpful and used it as a guide to prepare for my interview. I copied and pasted a list of TFA's core values and then started typing. As I began to list experiences from my own life in which I had exemplified those values, I had two overwhelming feelings. The first was that I didn't have a strong grasp of what each core value actually meant, and the second was that I wouldn't have enough examples to draw upon.

To ease the first feeling, I turned back to TFA's website. I remember thinking that the organization knew what it wanted in future teachers, and that all I had to prove was that I had those qualities. In order to convince both TFA and myself that I was what the program needed, I decided to be as honest as possible with my experiences. As an undergrad, I swam on a Division I swim team and ran a law journal. I was nervous that they wouldn't be enough, or that they wouldn't be perceived as the right kinds of experiences. But instead of making up a slew of leadership positions that I didn't have, I used those two activities and my roles in them several times over. I typed up every example I could think of.

When I felt that I could adequately represent myself as a person who lived TFA's core values, I started researching what the program actually looked for in candidates. I found an article that described just that and copied and pasted it into a Word document. When the article said, "We have discovered over time that these individuals [successful TFA teachers] exhibit a significant degree of leadership," I wrote down my own experience that matched it: *Law and Society Journal, editor-in-chief, managing 13 of my peers.* When the article said, "Some leaders are able to motivate colleagues and peers with an inspirational vision," I again wrote down my experiences as if the article had asked me a question: *Under my direction, we have expanded the journal to other UC campuses, and we're taking steps to encourage UC students of all majors to submit work.*

I then talked out almost every single answer I had written down with anyone who would listen. Sometimes it was a friend, sometimes my mom, and sometimes I just talked to myself to hear what it would sound like. Because I had done this, during the interview I spoke plainly and honestly, and I felt confident because the answers I gave were truly the best answers for me.

—Kaelan Dickinson (South Louisiana '09)

What to Expect

There are three components of the final interview: the five-minute lesson, the group discussion, and the one-on-one interview. You will be in the interview room with seven to twelve other applicants, and there will be two interviewers. You should get to the interview site at least 15–20 minutes early, although plan to be there 45 minutes early in case you hit unexpected traffic, can't find parking, or have trouble locating the interview room.

From the second you walk in until the second you leave, you are being evaluated. That means you need to stay professional and focused the entire time you are there. Do not assume that just because you are not teaching your five-minute lesson at that time, you are not being observed. The interviewers are watching how you respect and observe others. Stay engaged with the group and interviewers at all times and keep a positive and upbeat attitude. Simply being excited to be there can show your passion for the movement and desire to become a corps member. Keep your cell phone off and away at all times during the day, even when in the waiting room in the morning or during breaks. Speak professionally at all times, even if you know the interviewers or have friends in your interview group. If an interviewer hears you curse or speak in a derogative manner at any point, you likely will not be accepted.

Teach For America tells you to dress professionally. It does not elaborate on what this means, but there is only one answer: wear a suit—both men and women. Make sure the suit is clean, pressed, and fits well. If you wear anything else, you will have others around you who have taken the time and effort to look more professional than you. Do not let that happen.

Preparing for the Interview

You should prepare for the final interview in much the same way as you prepared for the phone interview. If you were invited to advance straight to the final interview and have not reviewed Chapter 9, "The Phone Interview," I suggest you go back and read it.

Obviously, the final interview has many more components and is in person instead of on the phone, so there will be some major differences. Here is a checklist of everything you should do before your final interview:

____Spend extensive time planning, preparing, and practicing your five-minute lesson.

___Review any articles or documents you received ahead of time and be ready to discuss them, including those from the online activity and phone interview.

___Continue anticipating questions and preparing responses about your resume, letter of intent, and personal experiences.

___Plan out exactly how long it will take to get to the interview location and know exactly where it is. If you are not sure, go a day or two early to familiarize yourself with the route.

___Review Teach For America's mission and practice talking about it in both short and long form.

___Upload one scanned official transcript for every college or university you have attended (when prompted).

___Upload photocopied documentation with proof of your identity and citizenship status (when prompted).

___Get a good night's sleep and wake up early enough to eat a healthy breakfast.

Once again, keep in mind that you are always being evaluated, from the moment you step in the door 15 minutes early to the moment you shake your interviewer's hand and thank him for his time.

Five-Minute Lesson

When you walk into the room, the interviewers will spend a few minutes introducing themselves. They will also make it clear that the applicants in the interview group are not competing directly against each other; rather, you are all being scored against a rubric that is used in all interviews across the country. Everyone in the room could get accepted, or none of you could get accepted. Because of this, all of the other applicants are generally supportive of each other during the lessons and will do what they can to help each other's lessons shine. Don't forget that *everyone* there is nervous, not just you.

The five-minute lesson is the first thing you will do when you begin the day after the interviewers introduce themselves. This inevitably causes the most stress and anxiety of any part of the Teach For America application process. Given that the vast majority of applicants are not education majors and may have never taught a group in a structured way before, this anxiety is perfectly understandable.

I'll give you a piece of insight: The five-minute lesson is the easiest part of the final interview because you have COMPLETE control over the entire process. You can practice the five-minute lesson until you can do it without even thinking about it. You can rehearse a live scenario in front of friends and then get direct feedback. You have unbelievable resources at your fingertips to help you develop your lesson (thanks, Google!) and plenty of time to perfect it. Plus, it is only five minutes long.

The first question I always get from applicants entering the final interview is, "What should I teach?" The truth is, it doesn't really matter what you decide to teach, as long as you can present it effectively in an organized and understandable way. I have heard of great lessons on microbiology and on recognizing the letter A. One of the applicants in my interview group did a lesson on the different kinds of electromagnetic waves (radio-waves vs. micro-waves vs. infrared waves, etc.). She was accepted. Find a topic that you are knowledgeable about and are comfortable presenting.

More important than the topic itself is being able to comprehensively teach the concept in less than five minutes (and as you will soon see, the actual instruction component will be much shorter than that). This means that you will have to narrow your topic to one specific concept or piece of knowledge. Instead of doing a lesson on the five-paragraph essay, you could teach how to create a thesis statement. Instead of a lesson on the American government, you could teach the concept of checks and balances between the three branches of government. In a real classroom, each of those lessons would likely come as one small part of a much larger unit.

When planning your lesson, be aware that five minutes *means five minutes*. The interviewers will cut you off mid-sentence if you run too long, so make sure that you can get through the entire lesson when practicing. This is actually a realistic expectation; as a teacher, you will have a specific time period in which you must teach a lesson, and you must be able to finish in that set time period every day.

I recommend planning to finish in 4 minutes and 30 seconds to give yourself a bit of leeway on time. It is likely that something will not go exactly the way you plan, even with plenty of preparation, and if you do finish 30 seconds early, you can always take an extra question from the group.

Planning the Lesson

The best way to prepare the lesson is through backward planning (which we looked at in Chapter 3). You will create the most effective lesson if you commit to aligning the outcome with your objective.

The most basic lesson plan format you will learn with Teach For America is the Five-Step Lesson Plan, which is designed to force you to plan backward. While you may not use this exclusively when you are actually teaching, it is a great first step and the best way to structure your five-minute lesson. Not only will it force you to stick to the point throughout the entire lesson, but it will also show the interviewers that you have done your research and can organize a lesson effectively. The five steps are:

- Opening
- Introduction to New Material
- Guided Practice
- Independent Practice
- Closing/Assessment

On the following pages, I have included a brainstorming worksheet and a lesson plan template to guide you through planning your lesson. They are designed to force you to plan backward and create a lesson that flows logically. Go through the brainstorming exercise and then fill out the lesson plan template. Regardless of the topic you choose, you are sure to create an impressive lesson that is organized and engaging if you use this approach.[1]

---

1 To download a PDF version of the brainstorming worksheet and lesson plan template, visit www.destinationteachforamerica.com.

Five-Minute Lesson Brainstorming Worksheet with Explanations

STEP	EXPLANATION	EXAMPLE
Step 1: State your objective · What do my students need to know/be able to do by the end of this lesson?	Your objective should start with SWBAT (students will be able to…). It should be easily measurable and contain only ONE specific concept that you want your students to learn.	SWBAT solve a two-step algebraic equation for x. *Note that there is a very specific skill (to solve) and a very specific concept (a two-step algebraic equation).*
Step 2: State why this is important and how it connects to a larger goal · Why should my students be learning this concept or skill? · What will it help them achieve in the bigger picture of their lives?	This should be something you can directly say to the class at the beginning of the lesson. You should mention how it relates to the larger unit AND something meaningful that expands beyond the scope of the classroom. Feel free to make something up for the five-minute lesson about how it relates to the larger unit in the class. It is OK to assume that students have prior knowledge on the topic.	"Learning how solve these types of equations is important for so many reasons. First of all, this is an absolutely essential building block for the rest of your time in math classes. Everything you do will have basic algebra involved in some way. "Not only that, but it's also important in real-life situations. What if you want to rent a bike and they charge you $10 plus $3.50 an hour? How much will it cost you to rent it for a week? You could use algebra to solve it in 10 seconds or less. That's the real value of this lesson."
Step 3: Create the assessment · How exactly will I know by the end of the lesson whether students have mastered this objective? · Does my assessment measure whether students know/can do precisely what the objective requires? · Is my assessment aligned with my objective?	In this step, you want to actually create the assessment that your students will complete at the end of the lesson. You are basing this assessment solely off your objective from Step 1.	**Assessment** Solve the following equations for x: 1. $4x + 3 = 7$ 2. $5 - 3x = 14$ *Note that this simple assessment is testing EXACTLY what I am planning to teach in my lesson and nothing more.*
Step 4: State the key points · What are the 1–2 most important things that students must know/be able to do in order to master this objective? · How can I state these in language that students will understand?	This is the trickiest part. You have to try to think about the concept from the students' perspective. You need to think about what kind of knowledge the students will be coming in with and the logical steps they must take to arrive at being able to successfully complete the objective. Again, you can assume that the students in your five-minute lesson have had previous lessons that logically lead to this lesson.	Prior knowledge: Students are able to solve one-step equations in all four operations. They also understand the order of operations. To understand two-step equations, they must: 1. Learn that algebra equations are solved by "undoing" operations in the opposite order. 2. Learn how to structure their steps by writing each step vertically underneath the problem.

Five-Minute Lesson Brainstorming Worksheet

Use the following template to do the preliminary planning of your lesson. For help, refer back to the explanations and examples on the previous page.

STEP	BRAINSTORM YOUR PLAN
Step 1: State your objective • What do my students need to know/be able to do by the end of this lesson?	
Step 2: State why this is important and how it connects to a larger goal • Why should my students be learning this concept or skill? • What will it help them achieve in the bigger picture of their lives?	
Step 3: Create the assessment • How exactly will I know by the end of the lesson whether students have mastered this objective? • Does my assessment measure whether students know/can do precisely what the objective requires? • Is my assessment aligned with my objective?	
Step 4: State the key points • What are the 1–2 most important things that students must know/be able to do in order to master this objective? • How can I state these in language that students will understand?	

Five-Minute Lesson Plan Template with Explanations and Strategies

Parts	Purposes	Possible Strategies
Objective	This should be something measurable and concrete. You should be able to say with certainty whether a student has learned the topic of the lesson. Take this directly from Step 1 of your brainstorming worksheet.	Start your objective with SWBAT (students will be able to...).
Key Points	From your objective and assessment, what are 1–2 most important concepts or pieces of knowledge your students need to learn to master the objective? Take this directly from Step 4 of your brainstorming worksheet.	Break down the objective into smaller pieces to figure out what these are.
Opening (20 Seconds)	This is your introductory statement or example to the students. Try to capture the essence of your objective in 1–2 sentences that explain the what, how, and why of your topic. If relevant, reference an imaginary previous lesson in which they learned something necessary for the lesson. It is perfectly acceptable to assume they have had a lesson leading up to this one.	Tell an anecdote, ask an engaging question, or share an interesting fact to connect the topic to the bigger picture.
Introduction to New Material (60 Seconds)	This is your "lesson" as you would normally think of a lesson. It presents a clear, concise explanation or demonstration of what is to be learned, but does not take a large chunk of the period. During the Introduction to New Material, you will teach your "key points" in a way that leads students to fully master your objective. Make sure to build a structured way for students to follow the lesson and check at least once that they understand the concept.	**Lesson** – Lecture, demonstration, presentation, graphic organizers, guided notes **Checking for Understanding** – Cold-calling, ask for response from each student on a 1–5 scale (1 = completely confused, 5 = understand entirely)
Guided Practice (90 Seconds)	This part of the lesson is meant to transfer some of the responsibility for mastering the objective to your students. Students attempt to explain or do what you have taught through an activity of some sort. It allows them to tangibly visualize the concept or practice it with coaching and guidance from you. Individual and group activities are both possible options.	Hands-on group activity, practice problems, discussion, graphic organizers, think/pair/share
Independent Practice (60 Seconds)	This is the time for students to practice completely on their own. This comes before the assessment, as you will be available to answer their questions and lead them to the correct answer. After they practice, you should quickly go over the answers.	Worksheets, higher-order questions, short-answer questions
Closing (10 Seconds)	This features a final check of what was learned, its significance, and its place in the larger picture. Usually, this is a VERY quick way to sum up the lesson by getting students to creatively describe it.	One-sentence summary from a student; ask students to connect it to their own lives
Assessment (30 Seconds)	This is the most important piece of the puzzle, because it's how you actually know if your lesson was effective and that students have mastered the objective. This should come from Step 3 of your brainstorming worksheet.	Exit slip, quiz
Homework	If you would like to create and hand out homework to show that you have come full circle in the lesson, you can do so.	Homework does not introduce new material. It should only provide additional practice.

Five-Minute Lesson Plan Template

Use this lesson plan template to create your lesson, based on the brainstorming worksheet you completed and the explanations on the previous page. When completed, this is your final lesson plan.

PLANNING	Objective	
	Key Points	
LESSON	Opening (20 Seconds)	Materials
	Introduction To New Material (60 Seconds)	
	Guided Practice (90 Seconds)	
	Independent Practice (60 Seconds)	
	Assessment (30 Seconds)	
	Pass Out Homework (Optional)	

Preparing and Presenting the Five-Minute Lesson

Teach For America is looking for proven leaders who are willing to adapt to their environment and continue to improve their skills. Keep in mind that you got to the final interview because you have many of the leadership qualities that TFA is looking for. From your application and phone interview, TFA gave you a score in a number of categories, and if your total score was high enough, you got to the final interview. The selectors have now given you the opportunity to show these qualities. Keeping in mind that TFA is looking for leaders, not just someone who can plan and create a beautiful lesson, will be important going into your final interview.

Your five-minute lesson can be about anything, as long as it is somewhat aligned with a subject taught at the grade level you specify. Remember that you need to show that you are a leader. Some people will come in with beautiful poster boards, creative games, small group activities, and more. These can be great (although they are not necessary), but they will work only if you can execute them effectively. So, whether you just use chalk to teach your "fifth-grade class" long division or give a little bag with pieces of colored paper to each applicant to teach your "first-grade class" about different colors, you should still aim to do the following:

1. Speak clearly, confidently, and use eye contact around the room at all times.

2. Ask questions of the other applicants, as they are your "class." Ask targeted questions to specific people throughout the lesson to make sure they understand the topic. This shows that you are leading and engaging your class.

3. Give your "students" 10–20 seconds to discuss the material in pairs at some point in the lesson. This shows that you are trying to engage your class in a way other than just asking for volunteers to raise their hand if they know the answer (you can do this after they have talked in pairs anyway).

4. Don't forget to ask your students if they have questions, whether it is during the lesson or at the end.

5. State your parameters and rules in about 20 seconds at the beginning of the class and write them on the board if you can. For example, explain that "students" are to ask questions by raising their hand quietly, or are to work in pairs by speaking to the person directly next to them.

6. Lastly, recognize that the TFA evaluators are also a part of your "class." They may ask a question during your lesson, so don't be taken aback or stumble if this happens.

—Abhinav Dev (Bay Area '12)

Group Discussion

The second part of the final interview is the group discussion. During this part, you will get into groups with other applicants and discuss a number of articles. Two of these articles will be the same ones you read for the online activity and phone interview. Thus, you should bring those articles and any notes that you took along with you to the final interview. A third article will be available to read in the Applicant Center before the final interview day. Spend time reviewing that third article in the same manner in which you reviewed the first two, and bring it along with any notes you took as well. Just like the first two, it will cover some sort of issue related to education and may refer to Teach For America's involvement in the movement.

As you read the third article and reread the other two in the days before your final interview, jot down notes about parts you think are especially important or arguments the author makes with which you either agree or disagree. At the end of each section and each article, if you have not already done so, write down a sentence or two outlining the author's main argument and your response to the argument. Think critically about what the author is saying, why she is saying it, and how you might be able to refute or support it. Think about personal experiences that may relate to the topic of the article and be ready to bring those into the discussion. Most importantly, think about how all three articles complement or contradict each other.

You will break into groups of three or four and spend half an hour or so discussing the articles with each other. You will sit around a table, and one of the interviewers will sit off to the side. The interviewers are not there to lead the discussion; they will simply be taking notes on the conversation. They are watching each of you closely to make sure you can contribute intelligently to the conversation without dominating it. You should be able to demonstrate that you can stand up for your beliefs, but are not so stubborn that you cannot listen to the opinions of others.

This discussion helps the interviewers evaluate a number of qualities. The first is your ability to communicate with people you have never met, which demonstrates your interpersonal skills and ability to respect people from different backgrounds. They want to see how you are able to take ideas and run with them and how you are able to handle opinions other than your own. If you are too controlling in the conversation, you will be perceived as not working well with others. If you are too quiet or let yourself get pushed out by the others, you may raise red flags about your interpersonal skills. You want to be someone with whom the interviewers would enjoy sitting down and discussing education policy.

The other important quality is your ability to think critically and organize your thoughts into clear and concise arguments. While reading, you should start to think about ways you may respond to anticipated topics, and you should be able to present them to the group in an organized way. As a teacher, you will spend a lot of time every day explaining concepts to students, and the interviewers want to see evidence that you can structure your thoughts.

You are likely to be a part of a group with one or more of the following three dynamics. Obviously, you have no control over who is in your group, but you do have control over how you interact with them.

The Balanced Group

The best group discussions are ones in which everyone is getting a chance to respond with equal frequency and all members are comfortable presenting their opinions and responding to each other. Everyone is willing to both take and relinquish control of the conversation as the discussion progresses. If this is your group's dynamic, be sure that you are an integral and engaged member of the group. At least once or twice, you should step in with a question for the group or with an idea that will take the conversation on a new path. If everyone in the group is on board with having a truly equal conversation, your interviewer will probably give all of you high scores, especially if the ideas presented by each person are really substantial. Keep the ideas flowing and keep smiling.

The Dominator

Many people who apply to Teach For America have strong Type A personalities. If there is someone in your group who is trying to absolutely dominate the conversation, do not battle her for the lead. It will not look good if you get drawn into an argument and lose your cool. Instead, be patient and wait for the discussion to go in a direction for which you have strong, meaningful input. When you speak, do so calmly, clearly, and with confidence. If you execute your input well, you will mark a striking contrast to the aggressive attitude of the other person. Make sure, though, that you do not let her completely push you out of the conversation. You must contribute to the discussion a number of times, or you risk coming across as a weak communicator.

The Quiet Group

Teach For America interviews are intimidating. Your group members may find it hard to get the conversation going, and there might be a lull in the beginning. If you feel like the members of your group are going to be especially quiet and passive, you have walked into a great opportunity to demonstrate your leadership ability. Take the role of the leader in the group, but do so in a way that does not overly control the conversation. Propose questions to the group and let everyone respond to them. If other people follow up with more questions, that's great. Respond to their questions. If the group gets quiet again, shoot out another question. If you can do this effectively, you are showing the interviewer that you can take control of a group and lead them in a meaningful way. Do not try to create this situation if it is not there, or you risk becoming a "dominator" in the discussion.

The group dynamic will most likely be some blend of these three scenarios. There will probably be some uncomfortable or less than ideal moments, and the whole point of the exercise is to see how you react on the fly. Treat others with the same respect you would expect from them, give quality input, ask thoughtful questions, and keep smiling. Make sure to be a valuable, but not dominating, member of the discussion. If you can do all of this, you should excel in this part of the interview.

One-on-One Interview

The last part of the final interview is the one-on-one interview, which is similar to any standard job interview for the most part. You will spend 30 to 45 minutes speaking with one interviewer. After the five-minute lessons and the group discussion, you will sign up for final interview times and then go to lunch. Your final interview may be right after lunch, or you might have to wait a few hours. If you are completely free for the rest of the day and someone else has a conflict that afternoon, defer to a later interview time. You will be demonstrating flexibility and have more time to collect your thoughts and prepare.

The most important thing to remember is to stay calm and confident. Make sure to maintain eye contact, keep your voice at a comfortable speed and pitch, and smile warmly. If you have interviewed with other companies or organizations or done interview preparation at your school, you will have an advantage because you will be more comfortable answering questions about yourself and your leadership experiences. Again, remember that Teach For America loves quantitative data and measurable results, so always try to draw the question back to an achievement for which you can concretely express your success.

Just as with the phone interview, there is no way to predict the actual interview questions, but there are some general themes likely to be included, so you should draft responses to the questions listed below. Brainstorm your answers, refine them so that they most effectively represent your accomplishments, and then rehearse them in front of a mirror and in front of friends. Answer them honestly and to the best of your ability. Stay confident and concise and speak about the quantitative outcomes you obtained, just as you did in your resume, your letter of intent, and your phone interview (if you had one).

Here are some questions for which you should prepare responses:

- Why do you want to join Teach for America?

- Tell me about yourself.
- What is the most difficult situation that you have had to handle?
- What is your greatest weakness, and how have you worked to overcome it?
- How do you prioritize responsibilities?
- How do you stay organized?
- What is your most significant accomplishment?
- Have you ever missed a deadline?
- What would cause you to quit Teach For America if you were chosen?

Let's go back to the newspaper editor we have been discussing throughout the book and look at how she might respond to a potential question.

Interviewer: "Tell me about a time when you missed a deadline and what you did about it."

Editor Candidate: "Well, let me tell you about the very first deadline I had as an editor. My style was somewhat more demanding than that of the previous editor, as I was determined to expand our circulation downtown and knew the paper had to improve to get us there. The night before that first deadline, we weren't even close. We got to 10:00 p.m. and still had sections that were unfinished, in part due to confusion regarding staff assignments. By midnight, I knew there was no way we were going to make it, so I decided to cut out the two sections that were holding us back, just for that day, so that we could get the paper out the following morning.

"I learned a lot from that first deadline and spent the entire next day developing a really solid plan to make sure such a delay never happened again. I allocated very specific responsibilities to individual people so that everyone would know exactly what they had to do. That week, I also wrote a guide that explicitly answered many of the questions that my page editors asked that night.

Everyone learned their responsibilities quickly, and we never had to cut out a section again. Now, I'm not saying we were never in crunch time again, but strong planning always ensured that we met our deadlines. As you know from my resume, we were then able to increase circulation of our paper by 65 percent by lobbying City Council to let us place stands downtown."

The editor did a number of great things in her response here. First, she directly answered the question by acknowledging that she had really messed something up. Everyone has missed a deadline at some point, and it is good to acknowledge that failure. Next, she mentioned that she quickly assumed control because she was determined to do something ambitious. Third, she talked specifically about what happened and, more importantly, about making an executive decision by a certain time to make sure the whole paper didn't miss the deadline, just those two sections. Obviously the newspaper ended up missing something, but at least they had a paper to put out. Next, she talked about not only what she learned, but also what she did *immediately* to remedy the situation. Within a week, she had an entire framework set up to ensure they were never in the same situation again. Finally, she threw in the result of the ambitious goal she had set by stating exactly how much she increased circulation.

My guess is that the interviewer's next words would be something like: "Wow, yeah, I was really impressed when I read that on your resume. Why don't you tell me a little bit more about your experience with City Council and expanding circulation?" She has just led the interviewer to ask her about arguably the most impressive part of her resume.

Role-Playing

One part of the one-on-one interview is a role-playing scenario. While it is a relatively small part, it is very important and can be one of the most difficult parts of the whole application and interview process. You will take the role of a teacher, and the interviewer will take the role of an administrator, coworker, parent, or someone else with whom you might interact when you are teaching. You will read a scenario and then act as if you are in a meeting to discuss the situation. The scenario will likely be similar to what you will encounter frequently when teaching.

Here is an example of what a role-playing scenario might look like:

Sample Situation 1

You are halfway through the year in your high school geometry class and have gotten into a great routine in your classroom. Students come to class on time, know the daily schedule, and are showing strong progress. Your students' average proficiency scores on state tests are higher than those of students in all of the other geometry classes, except the honors class. Although you have some students who are very advanced and others who are somewhat behind, virtually all of your students are improving.

Your principal calls a meeting with all of the geometry teachers and tells you that, starting in two weeks, any students who are behind in multiplication or division will be switching out of your class to one with a scripted curriculum to help remediate in these areas for the remainder of the year. This will count as their geometry credit. After the announcement, you ask your principal for a private meeting to discuss this further, and he agrees.

The role-playing is designed to measure how you react to difficult discussions. When thinking about how you will approach your situation, put yourself in the shoes of both the teacher and the person with whom you are interacting. Try to make the discussion genuine; act in a manner in which you would expect to act if it was a real situation. Speak clearly, professionally, and confidently, and always maintain the utmost respect for the other person.

There are a number of strategies that you can take when approaching the role-playing, but it is most important to respectfully stand firm in your beliefs and be passionate about your cause. In the case of Sample Situation 1 above, you have the right as a teacher to question the decisions made by the administration, and you need to be prepared to fight for what you believe is best for your kids. You do not want to be unreasonable in your demands, but make sure you do not easily take no for an answer. To display your potential for leadership, make sure to explain your reasoning in a manner that helps the principal understand your side of the situation.

You also never want to argue just for the sake of arguing. The goal is to reach a compromise that will ensure that your students receive the high-quality education that they deserve. Stand firm in your beliefs but make sure that you can recognize a compromise that will satisfy the end goal. As mentioned throughout the book, a true leader is able to bring others to his side because they want to be there, not because he forces them to be there. You never want to attack the interviewer personally or say anything negative. Respect for your colleagues, students, and environment is one of those seven qualities that Teach For America selectors look for; ignoring it will send off red flags. The interviewer is looking for persistence and leadership, so give them to him.

Five sample role-playing scenarios are included below, including Sample Situation 1 from above.[2] Sample Situation 1 includes an example of what the dialogue might look like between the interviewer and the applicant. It exhibits the types of interactions that might occur and how to handle a variety of questions from an interviewer. Your role-playing could be about this long, longer, or shorter; it depends on the interview.

I want to point out that this dialogue is meant to exhibit just one way in which a candidate could respond, but this is not necessarily the only way to interact. Do not simply memorize this dialogue or use it as a steadfast guide; rather, use it to craft your own voice and discover how you can display leadership in this activity.

Two important observations should be noted when reading through this sample. First, notice how the interviewer never simply says yes to the applicant. Most likely, you will have to keep responding to variations of "no" answers. Second, notice how the teacher continues to acknowledge the concerns of the principal but responds firmly and respectfully to explain her vision in each case. While she compromises, she never accepts "no" as an answer.

---

2 These are real situations that I observed and experienced when I was teaching. They have no relation to the role-playing scenarios that Teach For America creates. Any similarities between these sample scenarios and the one you receive during the final interview are purely circumstantial.

When you are finished reading through the sample dialogue, grab a partner and practice being both the interviewer and the applicant in the other three scenarios. It will be helpful if your partner has also read through the sample dialogue.

Sample Situation 1

You are halfway through the year in your high school geometry class and have gotten into a great routine in your classroom. Students come to class on time, know the daily schedule, and are showing strong progress. Your students' average proficiency scores on state tests are higher than those of students in all of the other geometry classes, except the honors class. Although you have some students who are very advanced and others who are somewhat behind, virtually all of your students are improving.

Your principal calls a meeting with all of the geometry teachers and tells you that, starting in two weeks, any students who are behind in multiplication or division will be switching out of your class to one with a scripted curriculum to help remediate in these areas for the remainder of the year. This will count as their geometry credit. After the announcement, you ask your principal for a private meeting to discuss this further, and he agrees.

Interviewer:
(As the principal)

So, you are concerned about some of your students switching to this new curriculum, am I correct?

You:
(As the teacher)

Well, first of all, I just want to thank you for taking the time to hear my concerns. I understand the need to help our students improve their multiplication and division skills, but I'm really concerned that we are setting them up to fail down the line by not teaching them the geometry that they will need in the future, especially for the SAT and in college. My lower-performing students have just been performing so well lately. Kids who came into my class the first day saying they hated math are now demonstrating dramatic improvements in math for the first time. While they may still be behind, they are *really* learning.

Interviewer: I understand your concerns, but geometry just isn't important if the students don't know basic multiplication tables. Plus, these students have learned the basics of geometry in the first half of the year with you already, so they at least have some of the skills needed for the future.

You: In terms of what they have already learned, yes, they have built a strong basic foundation, but they will not be ready for the future if they don't really learn the subject. Here's how I see it: Basic math skills are undoubtedly important for our students to learn, and it is unfortunate that many of the students have fallen behind. I don't think switching to a curriculum that is designed solely to teach these skills is the only way they can learn them, though; I think they can learn these skills within the current curriculum as well. I am concerned that if we pull the kids out of something they have begun to embrace, this is going to fuel apathy among these kids. I don't want this to hurt our students' motivation to learn.

Interviewer: Well, first of all, this new curriculum is designed to help students feel small successes, which has proven to help students stay motivated. And second, it's the responsibility of the teacher to engage students in whatever they are teaching—you know that.

You: Undoubtedly it is, and I have worked hard to instill that in my class. Even with students who are behind in many areas, my test scores show how much my kids are learning geometry. I have an idea that might allow me to keep teaching geometry to all of my kids but still remediate with students who need it. What if I took a look at the new curriculum and integrated the concepts into my lessons? I can target all students who need extra help and build a curriculum for them from the scripted one. They've already bought in with me, and if I explain to them the situation, I have no doubt they will be on board.

Interviewer: All right, I'll give you a copy of the curriculum this afternoon, and you can see if you can work it in over the next two weeks. I'll also come to visit your class at least once during that time. We'll re-evaluate in two weeks and go from there.

You: I really appreciate you listening to my concerns. I look forward to reporting back in the coming weeks. Thanks again for agreeing to meet with me.

Sample Situations

Sample Situation 2

You are in your second month of teaching fifth grade, and your students have finally started to engage in class. You spent the first two weeks mapping out the year and setting a big goal with your students. They just got their unit 1 test back and are excited and eager to move on to unit 2. One student in particular, Danielle, who has a history of failing grades and suspensions, has connected with you and is showing major improvements. Your principal calls you down to her office and explains that, because of scheduling issues, she is switching you to the third-grade classroom starting next week, and the third-grade teacher will be taking over your fifth-grade class.

Sample Situation 3

You have a first-grade student, Racquel, who is exhibiting signs of a learning disability, and you refer her to the school psychiatrist. Upon initial evaluation, the psychiatrist determines that Racquel may indeed have a learning disability, and you are assigned as the teacher to work with her and her family. You call her mother to explain the situation, but she has significant concerns about the school continuing to evaluate her daughter in this regard. She does not want Racquel to be labeled as "different" and fears that her daughter will be ridiculed at school if placed in special education classes. You know how important it is to have the parents involved, as well as how important it is to start working with Racquel while she is still young. You arrange an in-person meeting with Racquel's mother to discuss these issues.

Sample Situation 4

You teach eleventh-grade English and have been integrating SAT questions into your lessons to help prepare students for the test. You have found, however, that many of the students do not know how the test works and are eager for more help. You decide to start an SAT class after school, two days per week, to teach students SAT strategies. You get 15 students to sign up and submit a proposal to your principal. A week later, your principal informs you in a meeting that he will not approve the class, citing two reasons:

1. There are not enough security guards in the building during after-school hours.

2. This opportunity was not opened to all teachers. Because you will be paid overtime, the collective bargaining agreement prohibits him from authorizing the class unless the position is offered to all teachers. Just as for all after-school programs, the most senior teacher that applies must be selected.

Sample Situation 5

It is March, and student John switched into your English 3 class two weeks ago. Scheduling issues forced him to switch to your class from the English 3 class of another teacher, with whom he got along very well. He is an above-average student who enjoys participating in class and showing other students how smart he is, but you are having trouble getting him to follow the rules of your classroom. Over the past two days, he has been shouting out in class about how he "hates" your class because of your rules and how he wants to go back to his old class. You assign him detention for that afternoon and plan to talk to him in depth during that time about how he can become a positive member of the classroom.

At the end of the one-on-one interview, after asking your interviewer questions that you have for him (see Chapter 9 for advice on developing those questions), stand up, smile, look him in the eye, firmly shake his hand, and thank him for the opportunity to interview. You have now completed the final interview. You will walk out of the room both relieved that it is over and anxious to hear back.

Immediately when you get home, send your interviewer a follow-up email, thanking him for taking the time to interview you. Personalize the note with something that you enjoyed about the final interview. For example, you could mention how stimulating it was to have a discussion on education policy with the other candidates or how the five-minute lessons really got you excited about teaching.

In two to three weeks from your final interview, you will receive an email from Teach For America with your final admission decision.[3] If you are accepted, Teach For America will notify you as to which location, subject, and age group you have been assigned. Unfortunately, the admissions team does not give applicants who are not accepted any feedback as to the reasoning behind the decision.

---

3   If you apply at the November deadline, your notification will be in approximately two months because of winter break.

Chapter 12

I Got Accepted! Now What?

The day has finally come. You wake up in the morning and check your email. At the top is an email from Teach For America. You can see the first line of text in the preview. It starts with, "Congratulations, we are excited to inform you that you have been accepted…"

You have made it. You worked tirelessly through college to gain all of the skills and leadership experiences you needed to become a high-quality applicant. You wrote a stellar letter of intent, developed a resume full of your leadership experiences with measurable results, completed an online activity, went through an awkward 30-minute phone interview, and shined throughout the final interview. The journey has just begun.

As mentioned above, your acceptance letter will include your placement region, as well as the age group and subject that you will teach. For example, you may be selected to teach middle school science in Miami. Barring any extraordinary circumstances, you will not be able to change this assignment, especially the city in which you are placed. Thus, your decision to accept includes not only accepting a place in Teach For America, but also agreeing to move to the region in which you are placed.

You have to decide if you are willing to take the plunge into what will likely be both the hardest and the most rewarding two years of your life. You have to decide if it is worth being terrible at something for a little while and working more than 80 hours per week to figure it all out. You have to decide if you want to put off that acceptance to Columbia Law School or offer from JP Morgan to pursue two years of teaching elementary school. If you are planning to begin a career in education regardless, you have to decide if you want to begin by teaching in a low-income school that is often stretched thin. You have to decide that you are going to put your heart and soul into it and never stop working for the children while you are in the classroom.

Once you are accepted, you will have approximately two weeks to accept the offer. During those two weeks, staff members from the regional office of your placement city will call you to answer any questions or address any of your concerns. As Teach For America has spent countless hours interviewing you and poring over your application, and has finally decided that you will be an exceptional corps member, its staff will pressure you to some degree into accepting the position.

Don't be shy about asking them questions. Accepting the offer is not something to be taken lightly, so you want to be sure that you are entirely informed and comfortable with the decision you are about to make. Ask logistical questions about the region and the city. Ask about the support you will receive, both from Teach For America and from the school district. Ask questions about getting certified in the state and partnerships for certification and master's degrees. Ask about the stability of the school district in which you will be working and the most likely scenario for your placement. Ask if most corps members are placed in public or charter schools. Ask if you are more likely to be in a school with other corps members or be the only corps member in your school. Ask about average transition costs, including testing and paperwork fees. Most importantly, ask what the most successful corps members have done to prepare for the corps and develop as a teacher. This is your chance to ask anything and everything you want to know.

If you are accepted by Teach For America, I encourage you to accept the position. Ultimately, it is your decision, but the kids need you, and the nation needs you. You are undoubtedly capable of leading kids to success and becoming a part of the movement to reform what is the greatest civil rights issue of our generation.

Afterword

I close this book with a quote by William James, a nineteenth-century American psychologist and philosopher. It is a quote that I constantly reflect upon in my own life. The message holds true in classrooms, other professional endeavors, and personal relationships. Depending on the situation, it can help you build the courage to accomplish remarkable tasks or humble you when facing difficult decisions.

"Act as if what you do makes a difference."

Today, there is a critical problem in education in America. By choosing to apply to Teach For America, you have taken the first step in helping to lead the charge to end educational inequity, and your actions will make a difference.

When applying, inject passion into your letter of intent and walk into the interviews radiating that fervor. Make sure that you present yourself as a leader through and through, and that you are the best-prepared applicant in the interview room. If you do all of this, you have a great chance of getting accepted into Teach For America.

If you join Teach For America, do so with confidence, energy, and excitement. When you begin your training at Institute, enter with curiosity, determination, and dedication. Work harder than you ever have before so that you can learn as quickly as possible. When you begin teaching in the fall and have your first class of students, put your personal ambition to the side and dedicate yourself to your students. Model what you teach, act in a fair and honest manner, and respond to problems with flexibility and compassion. Get to know your students, their families, and their communities—and lead those who influence your students most to help you in your mission to educate them. Do absolutely whatever it takes to ensure that you are able to give your students the education they deserve.

Push your students to work harder than they ever have before and never back down from expecting the best from them. Show them that you are being so relentless because you care about them. They will get frustrated, they will throw fits, and they will want to quit, but when everything finally clicks months down the road, it will all be worth it. By the end of the school year, you will feel like you went to hell and back with some of your students, but they will come out better and more prepared for life because of you. Some of them will thank you, while others won't see what you did for them for years down the line. That's the reality of life as a teacher.

Regardless of what you believe, when you walk into the classroom on day one, you are not yet an expert teacher and will not be one for quite some time. If you have a question about how to teach a concept, how to set up your classroom, how to work with a difficult parent, where to find additional resources, or simply how to get a bathroom key, you need to ask someone in the school who does have that experience. Many veteran teachers have mastered their craft and would love to help an excited young teacher learn the ropes. If you go in with arrogance, you could alienate the very people who will be your greatest resources. Go in with an open mind, expect to fail, and always show that you are working hard to improve. The people who matter will appreciate it and work hard to ensure that you succeed.

So, get out there and show Teach For America that you know you can—and that you will—make a difference in the lives of children who need you most.

Appendix 1: Book Recommendations

Education

- Class Warfare; Inside the Fight to Fix America's Schools *by* Steven Brill (Simon & Schuster, 2011).

- Feel-Bad Education; and Other Contrarian Essays on Children and Schooling *by* Alfie Kohn (Beacon Press, 2011).

- Letters to a Young Teacher *by* Jonathan Kozol (Crown Publishers, 2007).

- Relentless Pursuit; A Year in the Trenches with Teach For America *by* Donna Foote (Alfred A. Knopf, 2008).

- Stray Dogs, Saints, and Saviors; Fighting for the Soul of America's Toughest High School *by* Alexander Russo (Jossey-Bass, 2011).

Poverty/Race

- Child Poverty and Inequality; Securing a Better Future for America's Children *by* Duncan Lindsey (Oxford University Press, 2009).

- I'm Not a Racist, But... *by* Lawrence Blum (Cornell University Press, 2002).

- On Race *by* Howard Zinn (Seven Stories Press, 2011).

- Traveling Light; On the Road with America's Poor *by* Kath Weston (Beacon Press, 2008).

- Whatever It Takes: Geoffrey Canada's Quest to Change Harlem and America *by* Paul Tough (Mariner Books, 2009).

- Why Are All the Black Kids Sitting Together in the Cafeteria? *by* Beverly Tatum (Basic Books, 2003).

Appendix 2: Sample Letter of Intent

- Why do you seek to join Teach For America?
- What would you hope to accomplish as a corps member?
- How would you determine your success as a corps member?

My goal in joining Teach For America is to be a superhero for kids who need it most. From a young age, I looked at my teachers as superheroes; they were people who had dedicated their lives to educating the next generation. They instilled in me an intellectual enthusiasm that inspired me to look forward to that next book on my reading list or my next science lesson. My teachers did everything that they could to ensure I got as much out of school as possible. Many of the students that Teach For America serves do not have the luxuries that I had growing up, but that does not mean that they should be denied an education.

I learned to love kids as a tutor at Washington Middle School, where I tutored two days per week during my junior year of college. While there, the teacher with whom I worked taught me how to use pedagogical methods and measurement systems to help students develop an intrinsic love for learning and, ultimately, succeed. The most important lesson that I learned is to involve students in all parts of their education, from planning long-term goals to measuring daily accomplishments. I intend to make that an integral part of my own classroom.

One of my eighth graders at Washington, Kayla, was struggling to understand why it was so important to learn math. One day, I pulled her aside for a conversation, and she told me that she wants to be a veterinarian. We then designed a project together that connected math to animals. She was excited about the project, and she started listening eagerly to her math teacher every day. She flourished in math for the rest of the semester. Before the project, she had a D average. Three months later, when the semester grades came out, she had earned a B.

This is the kind of accomplishment that I hope to realize as a Teach For America corps member every day. Ultimately, my students' achievements will tell me whether or not I have been successful in my role. If one of my second-grade students grows two years in her reading level during one year in my classroom, for example, I know that I have succeeded.

Education reform does not just live in the classroom, however. Teach For America's mission includes building a new set of leaders in education, people who will persistently chip away at the mediocrity that has plagued our underserved school systems. Joining Teach For America will allow me to meet people who can help me fight for systemic change in education. Whether I find my long-term career in the classroom or not, my goal is to join the struggle for educational equity for years to come. I know that Teach For America will give me the tools to make this a reality.

Appendix 3: Sample Resume

Jane Smith

123 State St., Los Angeles, CA 90001 • Phone: (555) 123-4567 • myname@college.edu

Education

University – *College of Arts and Sciences,* City, State   *Expected Graduation: June, 2013*
Bachelor of Business Administration in Finance
Major GPA: 3.85; Cumulative GPA: 3.68; Dean's List: 2009 – 2011, 2013
Semester Study Abroad in Rome, Italy
SAT Scores: Math: 720, Verbal: 690, Writing: 750
Presidential Scholarship recipient: sophomore – senior years, providing full tuition

Leadership Experience

Sample Sorority, *President* – City, State   *January 2012 – Present*
Managed 96 members of Sample Sorority, a national sorority renowned for its integrity, philanthropy, and high academic standards
• Maintain a yearly budget of $190,000, allocated between six position chairs including philanthropy, recruitment, and outreach
• Led communication with corporate sponsorships for major fall philanthropy event, raising $45,000 for cancer research
• Attend bi-monthly meetings with the Inter-Fraternity Council to discuss methods to improve Greek life on campus

Social Entrepreneurship Club, *Founder/President* – City, State   *December 2011 – Present*
University organization of 35 students engaged in social entrepreneurship strategy and implementation
• Since inception, members of the social entrepreneurship club have founded 6 social ventures that are all sustainable
• Run monthly meetings to foster collaboration among members and to brainstorm expansion options
• Recruit expert speakers to speak with club members about fundraising, strategic planning, and program development

John Doe State Senate Race, *Regional Field Director* – City, State   *May 2010 – November 2010*
Democrat successfully campaigned against 17-year Republican incumbent in largely conservative district
• Directed all campaigning on university campus and in surrounding neighborhoods on a $30,000 budget
• Post-election research showed that college-aged voters were a deciding factor in the outcome of the election
• Trained and managed more than 100 volunteers in door-to-door canvassing, on-campus flyering, and phone call strategy

Work Experience

Jones Accounting Firm, *Intern* – City, State   *June 2012 – August 2012*
Jones Accounting is a national leader in public audit services; ranked #7 company with which to begin a career by ABC Magazine
• Worked alongside a partner at Jones and a team of 6 on auditing a large healthcare provider
• Helped insure that sales of more than $2 billion were accurately accounted for according to new SEC regulations

Italian Restaurant, *Head Server* – City, State   *September 2009 – June 2011*
Popular Italian restaurant in heart of city commercial center with rotating seasonal menu
• Worked 35-40 hours per week to pay for tuition, room, and board
• Promoted to head server in September 2010; responsible for opening and closing each night, and managing 17 other servers

Campus Writing Lab, *Writing Tutor* – City, State   *August 2011 – June 2012*
Selected from 54 applicants for one of 10 positions as a drop-in writing tutor on-campus
• Advised college students on various stages of the writing process, including sentence structure and paragraph development
• Maintained consistent tutoring with 7 students; increased their average essay scores from a C to an A-

Additional Information

Skills: Microsoft Office, CSS Programing, database management, leadership, interpersonal communications
Interests: 5.0 level tennis player, concert pianist, travel, sports

Appendix 4: Sample Extracurricular Activity Submission

Organization Type
Athletic

Name of Organization
N/A

Please Specify
Varsity Basketball Team

Is/Was this a work role or an extracurricular activity?
Extracurricular

Number of people in this organization
25

If you lead/led people in this organization, how many?
12

POSITION

Title
Captain

_x_ I am/was a primary leader in this activity/job
___ I am/was a supporting leader in this activity/job
___ I am/was a general member of this organization

RESPONSIBILITIES & CONTRIBUTIONS

What are/were your primary responsibilities in your current or most recent role?

As captain of the varsity basketball team, I am responsible for leading my team during practice, during games, and off the court. During practice, I lead drills, work directly alongside my coaches to implement new workouts, and lead my teammates by modeling what it means to work hard. During games, I work with my coach to motivate my teammates, and I am the emotional and physical leader on the court. Off the court, I set an example for success by keeping my grades high and engaging in responsible behavior, and I encourage my teammates to do the same.

What has been your most significant contribution to this role?

Since I became captain of my team during my junior year, the men's basketball team has had the fourth- and second-highest-average GPAs of all athletic teams on campus. I am dedicated to ensuring that this academic success remains, and have arranged with my coach one additional study hall per week to help my teammates catch up on any missed work. We also won our conference tournament my junior year, and are currently ranked first in our conference (during my senior year).

AWARDS & RECOGNITION

Have you ever received a significant award or recognition in this role?

_X_ Yes
___No

Please list your significant award or recognition received. To list more than one award, click the **Add an award** link.

Award/Recognition:

Winter season student-athlete award

Briefly describe the criteria required to receive this award.

I was selected by the athletic department as a model of what it means to be an exceptional student-athlete at the end of the winter season during my junior year. To earn this honor, I maintained one of the highest GPAs among all athletes on campus and was recognized for my dedication to academics in addition to athletics.

PARTICIPATION

How many years did you participate in this activity?

Year 1	Year 2	Year 3	Year 4
_x_ First Semester	_x_ First Semester	_x_ First Semester	_x_ First Semester
_x_ Second Semester	_x_ Second Semester	_x_ Second Semester	_x_ Second Semester
___Summer Semester	___Summer Semester	___Summer Semester	___Summer Semester

Acknowledgements

First, I must thank all of my students who inspired me daily and led me to write this book. You are the future of this country, and without you, there is nothing to look forward to. Your energy and passion motivate me every day, and although I am no longer in the classroom, I will continue to do my part to ensure that your generation and the next receive a great education.

This book never could have been written without the corps members and alumni who lent their knowledge and advice. Special thanks are due to those who took time out of their busy lives to write candid and inspiring narratives, namely Geoff Kozak, Sara Kuzmik, Alyson Goodner, Abhinav Dev, Kaelan Dickinson, Bill Fickett, and Devin Potts. I also must thank the dozens of others who answered my endless questions in surveys and informal interviews, especially those of you whose responses ended up in the book.

My wonderful colleagues from Edison High School taught me how to teach to the fullest every day. Among countless others, Luli Demo (my co-teacher), Darryrl Johnson, Lawrence King, Stephanie Gaunay, Jason Carrion, Bridget Bujak, Lisa Kaplan, and Una Berry were instrumental to my development as a teacher. Your energy and passion kept me motivated to drive my kids toward success every time I stepped into the school. You are the GREAT teachers and administrators we talk about, and I know you will continue to have an enormous impact on your students for years to come.

I also have to thank the Teach For America staff who helped me along the way. Lance Tackett, you introduced me to Teach For America's high expectations in college by being relentless as a Recruitment Director. Sean Gustafson, you gave me your invaluable advice, strategies, and wisdom when things got tough as my Program Director. Ricky Cole, Tre Johnson, Dominique De Armond, and the rest of the Philadelphia staff, you have continued to support me in countless ways in the years since I left the corps.

Refining my book from initial draft to final printing has been exciting, humbling, and complicated all at once, especially for my editors and proofreaders. Thanks to Maddie Grant and my parents, Bruce and Ginny Whitman, for your initial edits and feedback. You were the first eyes on the book and gave me poignant opinions and criticisms when I needed them most. Thanks also to my editors, the magnificent Christopher Mote and brilliant Julia Kantor. Your disciplined minds were absolutely crucial for the finished product. For any other writers out there, hire these two immediately before someone else snatches them up!

I must thank the New Leaders Council for helping me develop my communications, fundraising, budgeting, and management skills, among so many others. Over the past two years, I have met and worked alongside dozens of amazing progressive entrepreneurs who are all fighting for vitally important causes. This incredible organization is enabling thousands of determined people nationwide to drive forward in their respective missions. I am forever indebted to NLC for what it has given me, and in awe of what it has accomplished in such a short time.

The lessons that I learned at my own high school, Walnut Hills, played a major role in developing my passion for education. I speak honestly when I say that it is the best all-around school in the country. However, a school is nothing without great teachers, and I absolutely have to thank two of my most inspiring teachers: Mr. Grunder and Mr. Martin. You both helped give me, as a teenager full of wild ideas, direction and confidence.

And finally, last but not least, I have to thank my family. Whitman and Conlan clans, you have given me immeasurable support in this endeavor and in everything else that I have done, and I can't begin to thank you enough. Most importantly, I have to thank my parents, Bruce and Ginny Whitman, and my brother, Andrew Whitman. You have stopped at nothing to guide me, encourage me, and support me. I love you more than words can express.

INDEX